Call of the Colorado

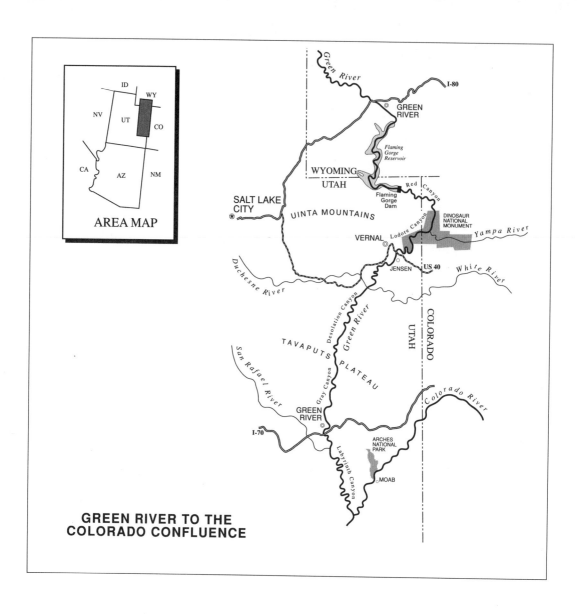

AREA MAP

GREEN RIVER TO THE
COLORADO CONFLUENCE

CALL OF THE COLORADO

By Roy Webb

University of Idaho Press
Moscow, Idaho
1994

Library of Congress Cataloging-in-Publication Data

Webb, Roy.
    Call of the Colorado / Roy Webb.
        p. cm.
    Includes bibliographical references and
index.
    ISBN 0-89301-161-4
    1. Colorado River (Colo.-Mexico)—
Description and travel.   2. Colorado River
(Colo.-Mexico)—History.   3. Colorado River
Region (Colo.-Mexico)—Description and
travel.   4. Colorado River Region
(Colo.-Mexico)—History.   I. Title.
F788.W44   1994
979.1'3—dc20   93-14424
                                        CIP

To
Dr. C. Gregory Crampton,
who got me started, and
Dr. Brigham D. Madsen,
who showed me how it's done.

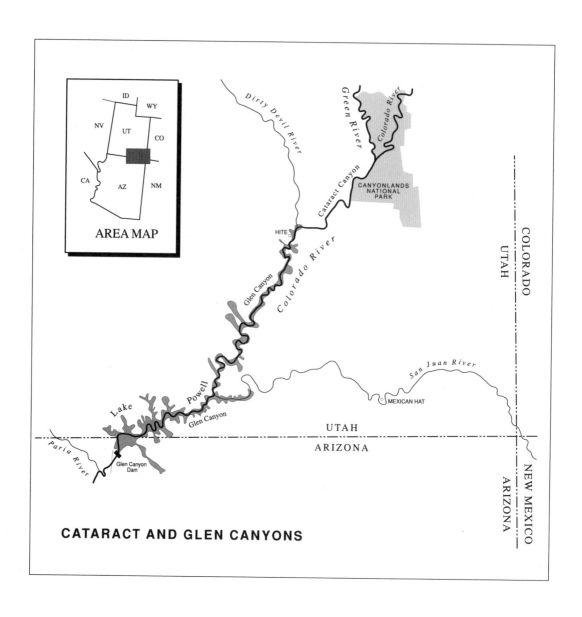

CATARACT AND GLEN CANYONS

As the day began, Siddhartha asked his host, the ferryman, to take him across the river. The ferryman took him across on his bamboo raft. The broad sheet of water glimmered pink in the light of morning. "It is a beautiful river," he said to his companion. "Yes," said the ferryman, "it is a very beautiful river. I love it above everything. I have often listened to it, gazed at it, and I have always learned something from it. One can learn much from a river."

—Herman Hesse, Siddhartha

CONTENTS

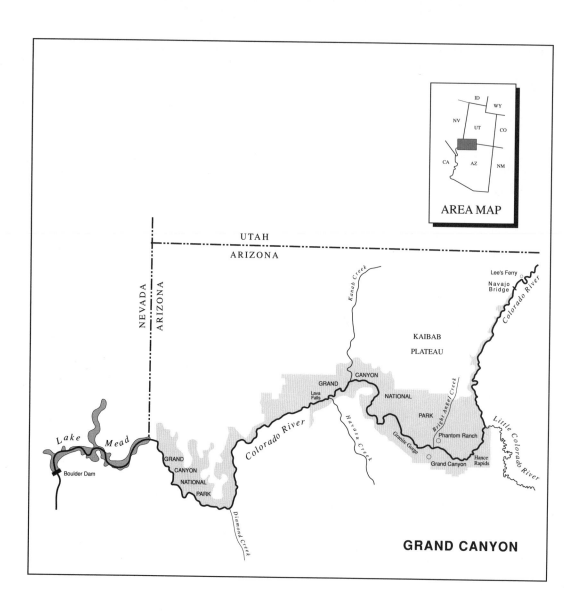

AREA MAP

GRAND CANYON

ACKNOWLEDGMENTS

The first time I ran Warm Springs Rapid on the Yampa River, in May 1980, I was cocky. I'd just come off a good trip on the Green River and had run every rapid successfully, and thought I had this boating business down cold. In Warm Springs—the biggest rapid on the river—after a cursory look, I got into my boat, missed my cut, barely got the boat turned in time to avoid flipping, and was thrown from the boat into the big hole at the bottom. It was one of the scariest experiences of my life, being sucked under water, bounced off rocks and shot to the surface, only to repeat the process several more times before I was washed up on a flat rock, sputtering, coughing, laughing hysterically. I was a changed man, and it was several years before I could row a boat again. Although I've run Warm Springs many times since, I've never approached it with that same confidence I felt at the top that first time.

This book, too, has its own history. When it was first written, during 1985 and 1986, I was riding the success (or so I thought) of my first book; even if it didn't sell a million copies it was a book, with my name on the cover, it was there in my hand. This current work was written while I was riding that crest, and I thought that I was going to go from one book to the next just like that. Alas, once again I missed the cut and was thrown from the boat. For one reason and another, the book was never published in that form, and it took me several years to get my confidence in myself as a writer and as a historian back. And I'll never again write anything from a newsletter article to a book manuscript without mentally preparing myself for that rejection slip that all authors know so well.

But all the while this book bubbled and gurgled at the back of my mind. I learned a lot about river history and even more about writing while I was doing it, and I always knew that there was a place for it somewhere. And now there is. There are many people to thank for this work, starting with those who saw me through the dark days after I washed up on my metaphorical flat rock, rejection slip in hand. First my irreplaceable wife, Becci, who never lost faith either in me or in the book. Next my life-long friend Mike Brown, with whom I've shared many rivers, many camps, many years. Other friends, colleagues, and river companions of those days: Rodger, Bobby, Bob L., Arnold, Reid, Dennis, Merle, Steve, and a lot of other people who listened to these stories told over and over and were polite enough, or sleepy enough, not to notice any variations in the facts.

Next comes Peggy Pace, whose editing and publishing skills have helped me through more than one rapid; she saw me through my first book, and wouldn't let me thank her then, so I insist on doing it now. It was her encouragement and interest in this book that saw it through to publication. My colleagues at the Marriott Library of the University of Utah have heard all these stories and more, and for years have covered for me when I was either searching out some obscure photo from a dusty archive, or off down the river somewhere to see it for myself. Greg Thompson, Nancy Young, Walter Jones; Mike, Jay, Paul, Ann Marie, Juli, Janet, Jennifer, Julie, and many more, colleagues of years now, decades even. Some of them I've even enticed down the river, and the rest know better, but thank you all.

And specifics: Sue Whetstone and Gary Topping of the Utah State Historical Society helped immeasurably with photos and manuscripts from their fine collections. Bill Slaughter of the L.D.S. Church Historical Dept. helped with materials from the papers of David Dexter Rust. Bud Rusho and Tom Friedman of the Bureau of Reclamation provided photos from their collections. William Jolley and Doris Burton of the Uintah County Library in Vernal assisted me in the use of the many resources in their fine Regional Room.

No book about the Colorado River can be written without a visit, or several visits, to the Huntington Library in San Marino, California, which houses the papers of Otis "Dock" Marston, and no research in the Marston papers is possible without the able assistance of William Frank, curator of Western Manuscripts. Mr. Frank prepared the finding aid (a book in itself!) for the Marston papers and has been unfailingly helpful in many other ways as well. William Mulane and Karen Underhill of the Cline Library Special Collections, Northern Arizona University, have helped with access to the marvelous photo legacy of the Kolb brothers and more recently, the papers of Georgie White. Also in Arizona, Susan Sato and Reba Wells, of the Arizona Historical Foundation in Tempe, assisted my searches in that institution and in other ways, as did Valerie Meyer of the Grand Canyon National Park research library. Finally, the staff of the excellent U.S. Geological Survey photo library in Denver, Colorado, deserve a vote of thanks and appreciation, as does Mr. Mastroguiseppe of the Denver Public Library for advising me to go there in the first place.

Besides the institutional sources, this book

wouldn't be as good as it is without the many people I've come to know on the river over the past decade. It's hard to remember everyone I've talked to over the past ten years and more that I've been researching and learning about river history. How do you credit the many riverside conversations, the shared pitchers of beer at Ray's Tavern, or the exquisite nights spent sitting on the boat after the passengers have been put to bed, listening to boatman stories as the stars wheel overhead and the river softly rocks the boat?

But there are some people I can thank for sharing their store of river lore with me: Bob Dye, Brad Dimock, Marc Smith, Don Hatch, Dee Holladay, Kim Crumbo, Vaughn Short, and Ted Hatch. The office staffs at Grand Canyon Expeditions, Hatch River Expeditions, and Holladay River Expeditions have answered many phone calls and questions and provided much information that has aided me greatly. For these people—and those that I've missed—my heartfelt thanks and appreciation; this is your book as much as mine. Finally I want to mention my two precious daughters, Rachel and Sarah; they give me hope for the future.

Roy Webb
Salt Lake City, Utah

INTRODUCTION

This is a book about a love affair, a love affair with a river, or rather two rivers, the Green and the Colorado. My affair with the Green River began during a summer spent as a seasonal employee of the National Park Service at Dinosaur National Monument. Like the New Yorker who never goes to see the Statue of Liberty, I lived less than forty miles away from Dinosaur for many years and had no idea of what lay beyond the swell of Blue Mountain. Once I realized what I had been missing, I lost no time getting acquainted with this wonderful region of cliffs and canyons and water.

Who were the first to see this land, I wondered as I floated along with the river rangers on their weekly patrols? What brought them here? What were their impressions? How did a voyage down "the Great Unknown" differ from a regularly scheduled patrol in a sturdy neoprene raft? Reading early accounts of the first explorers into the country around the Green River, I discovered that I was by no means the first to fall under its spell. People have long been moved by the rivers. They responded in different ways; some rhapsodized about the beauty of the canyons and the thrill of the rapids, while others cursed the rivers as having "generally more rocks than water." They may have cursed the river and the canyons—dragging a heavy wooden boat along the side of a roaring rapid lends a different perspective than running it in an inflatable raft—but they were all deeply affected by it.

Even though there are differences in the physical statistics of the Green and the Colorado—length, amount of water, drainage area—you cannot study one river without studying the other. Water murmuring past the riverbank on a moonlit night or the cottonwoods creaking in the breeze sounds the same whether you are in the Canyon of Lodore on the Green or Horsethief Canyon on the Colorado. The dip of a paddle in quiet shallows or the pull of the current on the oar in a rapid is identical, no matter which river you are on. The two rivers, then, are halves of a whole, and to learn about one is perforce to learn about the other.

Although the first explorers reached the Colorado only forty years after Columbus and the Green shortly before the United States was born, the first photographs were not taken of the rivers and their canyons until after the close of the Civil War. So this book covers the history of river travel from 1871, when the first photographs were taken with primitive, wet-plate cameras, to the early 1960s, when great dams were finished on both the Green and the Colorado, changing their character forever.

Geographically, this book covers the middle sections of both rivers: the Green from Flaming Gorge to the Confluence with the Colorado, and that stream from its source on the western slope of the Rockies to the end of the Grand Canyon. The upper Green and the upper Colorado haven't seen the numbers of people floating down the rivers that the above-named sections have, and so not much has been written about them. By the same token, the lower Colorado has been well known to travelers since the 1850s, and even had regularly scheduled steamboat lines plying its shores until after the turn of the twentieth century. That region deserves, and has had, its own books written about it.

Before 1950, fewer than a hundred people

had been down the Colorado through the Grand Canyon, and the same held true for other parts of the river as well. Until well after World War II, there were not many people on the river for the simple fact that it was hard to get there. Nor were there easily obtainable boats or outfitters who could take passengers. Now, however, that has all changed, and today there are many outfitters who take thousands of passengers yearly down the Green and the Colorado. Even though there weren't many river runners in those early days, it is impossible to portray them all in so short a work. Those chosen for this book are representative of the many others who felt the call of the rivers. For all those who were on the river, and I know there are many, many more—all those other scientists, prospec-tors, photographers, adventurers, and outfitters not included in this work—my apologies for not including them.

Just as we do today, so our predecessors had their own reasons for coming to the rivers. Some sought wealth in gold or furs or commerce. Others saw the river as a vast scientific laboratory, of a scale where the earth's very secrets are revealed. Not a few found the rugged country around the rivers to be a place of refuge from the pressures of society or from its laws. More important than the reasons why people felt the call of the river is the simple fact that they did. They came, they saw, they took pictures; and they were never the same afterwards. That is what this book is all about.

HISTORICAL BACKGROUND

Although the drainage basin of the Colorado River is one of the largest in North America, until relatively recently the river canyons were some of the least known. At the same time, the Colorado drainage was one of the first regions to be explored by the Spanish after their conquest of Mexico. This contradiction can be explained by geography. The drainage of the Colorado doesn't lend itself to settlement or even easy passage; the river can scarcely be navigated without danger, save for the stretch from near its mouth to the end of the Grand Canyon. Thus, the Colorado didn't provide any sort of avenue into the wilderness as the Mississippi did for the eastern United States or the Columbia for the Northwest. The Colorado has cut deep canyons that are quite impossibie to cross—even today there are only a handful of bridges that cross it or its sister stream, the Green River—channeling emigration routes and settlement into a few restricted locations. The land drained by the two rivers is for the most part arid, requiring intensive irrigation before it can be cultivated. The drainage basins of the Green and Colorado were simply not attractive to settlers heading west; they were just places to pass through to get somewhere else.

Even with these limitations, by 1540 the Spaniards had responded to the call of the Colorado River. That year Francisco Vásquez de Coronado and his lieutenants explored around the fringes of the Colorado's drainage basin. One of his men made it through the tidal bore at the mouth of the river and then 300 miles upstream, another crossed the Arizona deserts to a failed rendezvous above the mouth of the Gila River, and still another became the first European to see the Grand Canyon. Despite these incursions, however, Coronado left little lasting imprint on the Colorado Plateau.

The Spanish left the Green and Colorado alone for the next two centuries, even though they claimed as Spain's the drainage of the two rivers for the whole time. Their next *entrada*, in 1776, had more impact on the rivers. That year two Franciscan friars, Francisco Atanasio Domínguez and Francisco Silvestre Vélez de Escalante, were dispatched to seek a land route from Santa Fe, the capital of the Spanish province, to Monterey, the capital of Alta California. Working their way north through western Colorado, they crossed the Gunnison, a tributary of the Colorado above modern Grand Junction, and the main river a few days later. Reaching the Green above what is now Jensen, Utah, in September, they crossed by an ancient Indian ford and proceeded westward. Deciding to abandon the journey in central Utah, they recrossed the Colorado in Glen Canyon in the last weeks of 1776 and reached Santa Fe early the next year.

Their mission was officially a failure, but one of the members of the party, Don Bernardo de Miera y Pacheco, made an inaccurate map of their route that was the first to depict the upper basin of the Colorado. Miera's map would provide the raw materials for another made by the great German naturalist and explorer Alexander von Humboldt in 1811. Humboldt worked from a copy in the archives in Mexico City and so perpetuated Miera's mistakes. Besides the usual fantastic human figures and hopeful rumors of mineral deposits that always populate maps of the era, Miera depicted the Green (which Domínguez and Escalante had named the *Rio de San Buenaventura* as flowing directly west from northern Utah to the Pacific Coast. The myth of the San Buenaventura was not dispelled for another forty years.

Less than fifty years after the Spaniards had explored the basins of the Colorado and the Green, the first trappers entered the region. The first were British and Canadians, employees of the Hudson's Bay Company, who explored the upper basin of the Green as early as 1819. They were soon followed by Americans working for William Ashley of St. Joseph, Missouri. In the spring of 1825, Ashley became the first known person to descend the Green and leave an account of his passage, floating in bullboats from southern Wyoming to Utah's Uinta Basin. Ashley also established the name of the Green; before him it was known to Americans variously as the "Spanish River," the "Colorado River of the West," or the "Seeds-Kee-Dee Agie" (Prairie-hen River). Along the way he met a party of New Mexican trappers from Santa Fe who told him that they knew it by its Spanish name, *Rio Verde*—Green River.

Other trappers also explored the rivers around this time, although none left so detailed an account as Ashley. One was Denís Julien, a somewhat shadowy figure who made a number of voyages up and down the Green and Colorado in the 1830s. Julien is best known by the many inscriptions he left, ranging from a simple "DJ" in Desolation Canyon to an elaborate drawing of a boat and other symbols, along with his name and the date, in Labyrinth Canyon. A party of trappers led by Joe Meek, "the Merry Mountain Man," rode horses down the frozen river from Browns Park to the mouth of the White River, over a hundred miles, in the winter of 1838. Meek later tried to recruit vol-unteers to accompany him by boat down the river to California, but could find no takers. Farther downstream, James Ohio Pattie and his father Sylvester explored the course of the Colorado upstream from the Gila River as far as Glen Canyon in the late 1820s. Their account, however, is confused and disputed, and added little to the knowledge of the river.

By 1849, when the gold rush to California began, parts of the rivers were fairly well known to trappers, scouts, and government explorers, but not everyone had figured out that the Green and the Colorado were two branches of the same river system. It was common knowledge that the Colorado debouched at some point on the Pacific coast, but no one seemed to know just where. Even a little knowledge, however, was enough for some of the forty-niners, who wanted to get to California as fast as possible.

There were no doubt a number of unrecorded attempts to float the Green or the Colorado to California, but only one is well known to historians. William Manly and some of his fellow bullwhackers started down the Green from the Oregon Trail crossing in an abandoned ferryboat. They didn't get very far before the ferryboat was lost, so they made dugout canoes out of pine trees and continued as far as the Uinta Basin. There they met the Ute chief Wakara, or Walker, and on his advice abandoned the river and made their way overland to Salt Lake City. Manly's account of his voyage, *Death Valley in '49*, wasn't published until 1896.

The U.S. government finally sent official explorers into the region in the 1840s. One of the first of these was John Charles Frémont, who explored the area around the upper Green in 1843–44. Frémont finally determined that Miera's *Rio De San Buenaventura* was a myth after all and firmly placed the middle reaches of the Green and Colorado on maps. After the Mexican War and the Gadsden Purchase that followed it, the government began to take a greater interest in the Colorado River. Boundary surveys charted its course, and the first steamboats pushed up from the Gulf of California to supply the survey parties and their escorts. In 1851, Lt. Stephen G. Whipple of the Corps of Topographical Engineers ascended the Colorado from its mouth to a point above the Gila River.

The Utah War of 1857–58 was a further inducement; the army needed a supply point closer to Utah and less subject to interdiction than the overland trail. In 1858 Lt. Joseph C. Ives, who had been Whipple's assistant, took the steamboat *Explorer* up the Colorado through Black Canyon (where Boulder Dam now stands) to Las Vegas Wash. From there, Ives went overland, working his way around the south side of the Grand Canyon and down Diamond Creek to the river, becoming the first known American to reach the bottom of the Grand Canyon. After deciding that it was "an altogether profitless locality," Ives continued on to Santa Fe. His report seemed to sum up what had already been learned by Spaniards, trappers, and forty-niners: "It seems intended by nature that the Colorado River, along the greater portion of its lonely and majestic way, shall be forever unvisited and undisturbed."

It's not in the makeup of Americans to leave anything undisturbed for long, however, and the next year Capt. John Macomb was sent to find and plot the position of the confluence of the Green and the Grand (as the Colorado was then known). After struggling over fantastic humps and domes and ledges of bare sandstone, "impassable to everything but the winged bird," to within a few miles of the confluence, Captain Macomb and Dr. Newberry, the geologist accompanying him, gave up and turned back. They had gotten as far as the canyon of the Colorado and seen in the distance the gorge of the Green, so they knew where the two rivers came together. That was good enough for Macomb, who called the area "a worthless and impracticable region."

There were others—the railroad surveys of the 1850s, the Mormon explorers and colonists, more gold rushers—but Captain Macomb was one of the last to explore the region of the Green and Colorado before the Civil War broke out in 1860. For five long years, American energies were directed toward destroying each other instead of exploring "worthless and impracticable" parts of the country. Not long after the war ended, however, Americans were ready to take the unity and vigor developed in that terrible struggle and use them to start the conquest of something else—the Colorado River of the West.

CHAPTER I
Scientists, Surveyors, and Dam Builders

From the fabulous stories, the facts, and the reports, and from the knowledge of other cañons, I came to the belief that the "Grand Cañon of the Colorado" could be explored by descending the river in small boats . . .

Having made up my mind to explore the gorge, I came from the mountains to Chicago last spring, to procure outfit and build boats. Four of these were made on a model devised for the purpose of navigating canyon streams; and taking them out to Green River Station, where the Union Pacific Railroad crosses the Green, I was ready to embark. There I had a party of nine men awaiting my arrival, and anxious to enter the "Great Unknown" with me—men all experienced in the wild life of the country, and most of them in boating on dangerous streams.

—John Wesley Powell
in *New Tracks in North America*

Although government surveys had been exploring the fringes of the Green and Colorado country since the 1840s, it wasn't until a few years after the Civil War that John Wesley Powell, a veteran of that conflict, decided to explore the river itself. Starting in May 1869 from Green River, Wyoming, Powell and a grumbling crew of frontiersmen and "old soldiers" portaged, lined, and cursed their heavy oak boats down fifteen hundred miles of unknown river. One boat and three men were lost in the process, but Powell's systematic survey of the Colorado was widely heralded at the time and has become an epic of American exploration.

As much as he basked in the publicity and relished the appropriation from Congress to continue his surveys, Powell knew that not much scientific work had really been accomplished during the 1869 trip. Almost two years to the day after the first, Powell's second expedition left Green River. The second survey faced many of the same hardships, including arduous labor on short rations, but suffered none of the disasters.

In 1871, while Powell was still in the upper canyons of the Green, Lt. George M. Wheeler of the Geographic Survey West of the 100th Meridian and a crew of scientists, soldiers, and Mohave Indians dragged two boats up the Colorado River from Fort Mohave to Diamond Creek in the lower Grand Canyon. There Wheeler and the scientists left the party, "inordinately proud," as one historian put it, "of what was essentially a useless accomplishment."

The next surveyor to study the river was not a government scientist but a well-known railroad construction engineer. Robert Brewster Stanton was hired in 1889 by Franklin M. Brown, a Denver promoter and speculator, to be chief engineer of the Denver, Colorado Canyon, and Pacific Railway Company. Brown dreamed of a water-grade railroad along the bed of the Colorado from Green River, Utah, to southern California. Stanton, already an accomplished engineer, was to complete the survey along the bottoms of the canyons. After an almost unbelievable series of calamities, including the loss of boats and provisions and the drowning of three men in Marble Canyon (including Frank Brown), Stanton abandoned the river in late 1889. Amazingly, he was back shortly thereafter to complete the survey of what he had earlier referred to as "Death's Canyon." This he did, despite the loss of the photographer to a serious fall from a cliff shortly after entering Marble Canyon. After evacuating the injured man, Stanton taught himself to use the camera and pushed on, completing the survey without further disaster. By the time he finished, however, the investors had backed out, and the railroad was as dead as the unfortunate Brown.

By the beginning of the twentieth century, the seeds planted and nurtured by Powell and Stanton had begun to bear fruit. The U.S. Geological Survey was created in 1879 to coordinate far-flung government survey and scientific activities, and in 1902 the U.S. Reclamation Service was established. Within five years of its birth the latter agency began investigations of a potential damsite on the upper Green; 1914 found it doing the same thing at the confluence of the Green and Colorado. Although neither dam was ever built, the U.S.R.S.—which became the Bureau of Reclamation in 1923—has remained a force in western water politics ever since.

Before the new century was more than a de-

cade old, the U.S.G.S. began an intensive survey of the canyons of the Green and Colorado for damsites. Also involved were utilities such as Utah Power and Light and Southern California Edison. The U.S.G.S. was looking for water storage sites to fulfill the provisions of the newly signed Colorado River Compact, and the utility companies for hydroelectric potential; together their crews mapped, plotted, and located dozens of potential damsites on both rivers and on some of their tributaries. All of this activity culminated in the choice of a site on the lower Colorado for the government's first big project, Boulder Dam. After its completion in 1935, the Bureau and the U.S.G.S. directed their energies to rivers in other parts of the West. It wasn't until the late 1940s that the focus of the dam builders again centered on the Green and Colorado.

The Colorado River Storage Project was first introduced into Congress in 1946. This massive reclamation project, the largest of its kind ever proposed, called for at least five large dams on the Green and Colorado rivers as well as dams on most of their major tributaries. One of these, the Echo Park Dam, was to be built on the Green River in the middle of Dinosaur National Monument. The idea of a reservoir flooding most of a national monument set off a firestorm of controversy that eventually led to the Echo Park Dam being dropped from the enabling legislation. The defeat of the Echo Park Dam, however, didn't deter the Bureau for long. Planning for Glen Canyon Dam, Flaming Gorge Dam, and smaller dams on the San Juan, the Gunnison, and other tributary streams went ahead; by 1963 all were complete or nearing completion. The muddy, turbulent, unpredictable rivers that had so frustrated a generation of engineers, farmers, and advocates of land reclamation were no more.

Major John Wesley Powell, 1867

John Wesley Powell, ethnographer, linguist, geologist, visionary, was one of the first to recognize the need for land-use planning and government control of water reclamation in the West. He is better known today, though, for his two pioneering voyages down the Colorado River in 1869 and 1871–72. After the Civil War—undeterred by the loss of his right arm at Shiloh in 1862—Powell became a professor and led groups of students on field trips into the Rocky Mountains. During one such trip, in 1868, the idea of exploring the unknown canyons of the Green and Colorado by boat was born. Powell's first expedition, in 1869, turned into a race for survival. One of the boats was wrecked early in the trip, and the rest were reduced to battered, leaky hulks. At the end the men were living on coffee, "dough gods"—cooked lumps of moldy flour—and musty dried apples. Not much scientific work was accomplished, and three men who abandoned the river near the end of the Grand Canyon and climbed out were never seen again.

Two years later Powell took a different crew, consisting of close associates and members of his family, on the same trip. This time, however, he only went as far as Kanab Creek in the Grand Canyon. The 1871 expedition had its share of adventure, but was much more successful in scientific terms. The canyons were named, the river courses plotted; the first photographs of the river and the canyons were taken with an unwieldy wet-plate camera. After the river journey, Powell's crews spent the next several years surveying and mapping the rugged country of southern Utah and northern Arizona.

Later in life Powell was instrumental in the creation of the U.S.G.S. and the Bureau of American Ethnology, and became a recognized authority on the problems of water in the arid West. His could be a disagreeable genius, however; he was irascible, short-tempered, opinionated, and did not suffer fools. Those who knew him either worshipped or hated him passionately; there was little middle ground where Powell was concerned. He was so certain his pioneering voyage down the Colorado could never be duplicated that he spurned any later explorers who came to him for advice. But Powell also had a visionary, almost mystical side to his character. That this side of the one-armed genius was deeply touched by the Colorado is very evident in his report, *The Canyons of the Colorado*, published in 1875. Despite its inaccuracies and deletions, it is still regarded as one of the finest descriptions of the Green and Colorado rivers. Powell felt the call of the Colorado to the end of his days.

John F. Steward, Member of Powell's Second Expedition, in Glen Canyon, 1871

Steward was an amateur geologist who was engaged by Major Powell as an assistant for the Second Colorado River Exploring Expedition in 1871. Powell and Steward met during the siege of Vicksburg in 1863 while they were both looking for fossils in the freshly dug trenches. Steward was severely wounded in 1864 and mustered out of the Army. When Powell asked him to join the crew, Steward jumped at the chance for adventure and to serve under his old comrade once again. Unlike some other members of the second Powell expedition, Steward was down-to-earth, irreverent, and had a good sense of humor. Scouting a difficult rapid in the Canyon of Lodore on the Green, Powell called for suggestions for a name. The sober "Prof" Thompson and Francis M. Bishop both agreed on Boulder Falls. Powell turned to his old comrade Steward and asked what he thought. Steward looked at the narrow, rock-strewn channel disappearing around the corner of the canyon, thought about the arduous multi day portage that faced them, and replied, "Would Hell's Half Mile suit?" Suit the Major it did, much to the pious Bishop's dismay, and so it was named.

During the rest of the survey, poor food, cold weather, and the labor of lining and portaging aggravated Steward's old war injury so much that toward the end of the voyage he had to be carried on a stretcher. Steward resigned from the expedition when the party moved to Kanab, Utah, to establish winter quarters.

Frederick S. Dellenbaugh with the Flag of the *Emma Dean*, 1929

At seventeen years of age, Fred Dellenbaugh was the youngest member of the second Powell expedition. He went along as artist and assistant over his parent's objections, and in fact waited almost until he was on the river to wire them of his plans to accompany the Major. Dellenbaugh was entranced not only by the grand adventure he was a member of, but also by the stoic Major Powell, and greeted each new hardship or mishap as simply one more facet of the voyage. He stayed with the survey until 1875, spending the winters in Kanab, Utah, and the field season exploring and mapping the region around the Grand Canyon. He is shown here later in life, with the flag from Powell's boat, the *Emma Dean*. The flag was made by Powell's wife, Emma Dean, and Dellenbaugh was a member of the crew.

Like so many others after him, Dellenbaugh was forever changed by the river and the canyons; unlike many others, he was able to channel his obsession with the river to positive ends. Dellenbaugh became a widely known explorer, lecturer, and author and a founding member of the Explorer's Club. He wrote numerous books and articles, including an account of his voyage with Powell, *A Canyon Voyage*, and a history of the exploration and settlement of the river, *Romance of the Colorado*. He also became the chief apologist for Major Powell. Unfortunately, he carried his loyalty to Powell to the point of insisting that the names of the three crewmen who had left the 1869 voyage be omitted when the Powell monument on the south rim of the Grand Canyon was built in 1916—a disservice to brave men and to history alike.

The Start of the Denver, Colorado Canyon, and Pacific Railway Company Survey, July 1889

When Robert Brewster Stanton saw the boats that Franklin Brown, the company president, had ordered for the river survey, he was aghast. They were clinker-built (hard to repair), round-bottomed (hard to maneuver), "hunting and pleasure craft," completely unsuited for the turbulent waters and rocky channels of the Colorado. Worse, they were made of thin red cedar; two of them had cracked hulls just from being shipped to the river! Brown chose light craft in the hope of avoiding the onerous labor of portaging heavy oak boats such as Powell's men had endured. To compound his errors, Brown struck the experienced boatmen Stanton had recruited from the personnel list, replacing them with gentleman friends of his from Denver, and refused to obtain life preservers for the crew, eschewing the need for such unmanly aids.

Since all the provisions and instruments wouldn't fit into the boats, the food was stored in waterproof tin boxes that were lashed together into a raft. In the first rapid in Cataract Canyon, the raft came apart and most of their food was lost. Also lost in Cataract were two boats, smashed to splinters against the rocks. Brown's failure to provide life jackets was his most serious mistake, one which he paid for with his life in Marble Canyon. Also drowned a few days later were Peter Hansborough and Henry Richards, the latter attaining the dubious honor of becoming the first and possibly only black man to drown in the Grand Canyon. After Hansborough and Richards were lost, Stanton left the river, abandoning the worthless boats. When he returned to finish the survey the next year, he was equipped with sturdy oak boats and life preservers.

U.S. Reclamation Service Drill Crew at Head of Cataract Canyon, September 1914

During the late summer and early fall of 1914, a drilling crew from the U.S. Reclamation Service (the predecessor of the Bureau of Reclamation) spent two months investigating the site of a proposed dam just below the confluence of the Green and Colorado rivers, in what is now Canyonlands National Park. Led by E. C. LaRue, the crew drilled numerous test holes, trying to determine the suitability of the rock strata for a dam that would have backed the river up for hundreds of miles, flooding the towns of Moab and Green River, Utah. LaRue, a

U.S.G.S. hydrologist, was consumed with the idea that a high dam was needed on either the Green or the Colorado for flood control and water storage. At the end of September, inconclusive results and a sudden rise in the river that flooded the drill site—not to mention the difficulty of supplying a crew in the middle of nowhere—caused the abandonment of the project. Even though it was a good job, such a remote site was considered a real hardship tour. The nearest towns were Moab, about sixty miles up the Colorado, and Hite, about the same distance downstream. Supplies, equipment, and personnel had to be brought down the Green by boat from Tom Wimmer's ranch at the mouth of the San Rafael River, about a hundred miles one way. The trip usually took two days, although that could change with the level of the river; more water meant a faster trip while a lower river could mean adding considerably to the travel time. And it was brutally hot at the bottom of the canyon; there was very little shade and the work was hard. In the end, this survey came to naught, but E. C. LaRue went on to participate in other surveys of the Colorado in the coming years.

W. R. Chenoweth at His Plane Table in Cataract Canyon, 1921

In the fall of 1921, a joint U.S.G.S.-Southern California Edison survey party set out from Green River, Utah, to survey the lower Green and the Colorado for damsites as far as Lees Ferry. The party included Eugene Clyde LaRue, Sidney Paige, geologist, and Ellsworth Kolb as head boatman. They used three boats, two of them large Galloway-style skiffs and a third of different design, christened the "Tub" because of its odd shape. Also along, rowing his own boat, was Emery Kolb. Not an official member of the party, Emery wanted to photograph both the scenery in the Land of Standing Rocks and the boats running the rapids of Cataract Canyon. The crew was an experienced one: Chenoweth had completed a survey of the Snake River in 1920, and two of the crew members had been with him then; LaRue was a veteran of other U.S.G.S. river surveys in the canyon country; and the Kolb brothers had first boated the Green and the Colorado as early as 1911.

The group ran the upper part of Cataract Canyon without mishap, but in Dark Canyon rapid, one of the last in Cataract, Ellsworth Kolb ran into problems. He ran the first boat onto the rocks, where it was stuck for over a day; hung the second on the same rocks, although he was able to free it; and capsized the last in the giant tailwaves. Nothing was hurt, however, save for Ellsworth's pride and E. C. LaRue's cigars, which had been in the first boat and were ruined by the muddy water. Dark Canyon was reputedly one of the worst rapids in Cataract Canyon, but is now submerged under the waters of Lake Powell.

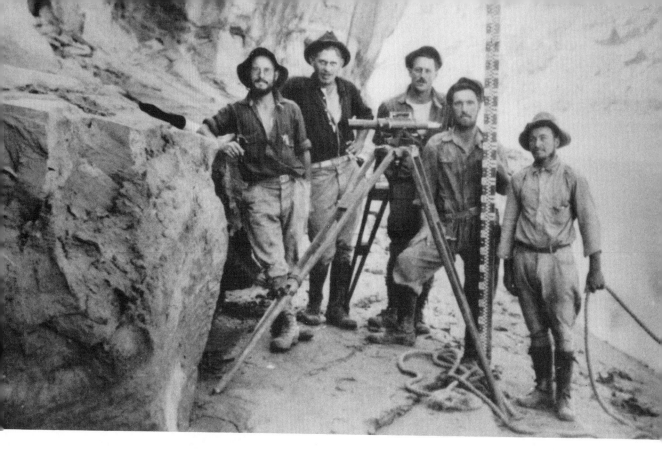

U.S. Coast and Geodetic Survey Crew in Glen Canyon, 1921

In 1921, the U.S. Geological Survey asked their sister organization, the Coast and Geodetic Survey, to establish a series of benchmarks on a line from Green River, Utah, to Flagstaff, Arizona. The benchmarks would be necessary for the U.S.G.S. survey of Cataract and Glen Canyons that was scheduled to begin later that year. The duties of the Coast and Geodetic Survey were normally to establish harbor locations, survey the magnetic field of the earth, and other more esoteric functions. In this case, though, they reluctantly agreed to help the U.S.G.S. Two separate parties started from the opposite end of the line, working toward each other. They were to meet in Glen Canyon at the Crossing of the Fathers. Both crews, however, unused to the difficult terrain and weather of the canyon country, met with more difficulty than they could have imagined and didn't rendezvous until November 11. The *Annual Report* for that year declared: "This line of precise levels is probably the most difficult one in the history of the U.S. Coast and Geodetic Survey . . . Many unusual conditions and difficult situations [such as a frozen river and howling windstorms] had to be met by unusual methods of leveling. . . . At best the work was extremely difficult."

Kelly Trimble, Topographic Engineer, at Work During the U.S.G.S. Survey of the San Juan River, July 1921

Although prospectors had been running the San Juan river since the early 1890s, the Trimble party of 1921 was the first to map and plot the lower canyons of the river and only the fourth to descend the river to its mouth in Glen Canyon. The crew consisted of Kelly Trimble, the leader; Hugh Miser, geologist; H. Elwyn Blake and Hugh Hyde, rodmen; Heber Christensen, cook; and Bert Loper, boatman. Robert Allen, the recorder, represented Southern California Edison. Christensen was also supposed to be a boatman, but he froze at his first sight of sand waves. Loper, disgusted with his performance, ran both the boats himself for most of the rest of the trip, with help from budding riverman Elwyn Blake. The survey party was in and around the San Juan from July to October, during the hottest part of the year. Not only were they to survey the river, but they also had to survey up to a certain level in the canyon, and as they got farther downriver they had to go farther and farther into the canyons to reach that level. Geologist Miser and Bert Loper—who had no duties other than running the boats—made side trips across the desert to places of interest as much as twenty-five miles away. Miser later wrote, "The voyage was attended by strenuous labors and hardships."

Bert Loper Running Slickhorn Rapid on the San Juan River, August 1921

By 1921, Bert Loper was known as one of the most experienced rivermen on the Colorado. He got his start on the San Juan during the gold rush of the 1890s, and later boated up and down Glen Canyon for many years. Bert was one of the first true river rats in the modern sense of the word; he loved the river, loved the canyons, and after his first trip on the San Juan never felt at home any place else. In 1921, the U.S.G.S. hired him to be head boatman for their survey of the San Juan River. Loper usually ran both of the sixteen-foot, flat-bottomed, open rowboats through the rapids himself, while the others portaged the supplies and surveying instruments. Occasionally, however, he would allow H. Elwyn Blake, son of an old river family, to run one of the boats. At a small rapid just above the mouth of John's Canyon, however, it was too hot to take the usual precautions, so Bert elected to run the boats through without unloading them. To everyone's dismay, one boat just missed the canyon wall, only to strike a boulder and "burst on one side from stem to stern. [It] nearly filled with water by the time a landing place was reached." Running rapids in the days before inflatable rafts was considerably different.

Taking It Easy Just Below Green River, Wyoming, July 1922

The survey of the Green River from above Flaming Gorge to Green River, Utah, was a joint effort of the U.S.G.S. and Utah Power and Light Co. Leigh Lint, here at the oars, was one of the boatmen; John Clogston, taking it easy on the stern deck, was the cook. Both were veterans of previous river surveys. They had served together on a U.S.G.S. survey of the Snake River in 1920. Clogston had also been with the Cataract Canyon survey in 1921. Other crew members were also veterans: Kelly Trimble, the trip leader; Bert Loper, head boatman; and H. Elwyn Blake, rodman and boatman. Ralph Woolley was the chief hydrologist and recorder, and a civil engineer from Salt Lake City, H. L. Stoner, represented Utah Power and Light and kept the expedition's books. Several other parties had already plotted parts of the river; the purpose of this expedition was to tie all the various surveys together. As recorder, Woolley later completed and published the first plan and profile of the Green River and mapped fourteen damsites during the two-month survey.

U.S.G.S. Crew at Lees Ferry, August 1923

The 1923 Grand Canyon survey came about partly because of politics. As specified in the Colorado River Compact of 1922, plans were made to build a big dam somewhere on the Colorado. California, with its much greater political pull, made sure the dam was to be somewhere on the lower Colorado so that the Imperial Valley and the city of Los Angeles could derive the maximum benefit from the dam's water and power.

It was an experienced crew, probably the best that could be had in the country at that time. Leigh Lint and H. Elwyn Blake both had been on previous river surveys, as had Emery Kolb; Lewis Freeman was also an accomplished riverman and a writer as well. He planned to write a book about his experiences on this trip and others. Conspicuous by his absence is Bert Loper, who had hoped to be the head boatman for this survey. Birdseye refused to hire him, citing his age (Loper was fifty-four) but the real reason was probably the bad blood between LaRue and Loper, resulting from a violent disagreement the two men had had in Glen Canyon two years before. Equally absent from this picture is Frank Dodge, who—even though he was probably a better boatman than any of them—was too late to get a boatman job and was hired as rodman and camp helper. According to Dodge's own story, he swam across the river to visit a friend, who gave Dodge some homemade fig wine. Too much wine, as it turned out, and by the time Dodge got back across the river it was all he could to make it into the shade and pass out.

Measuring the Flow of Deer Creek Falls, Grand Canyon, 1923

The Grand Canyon survey of 1923 was one of the best-equipped and best planned surveys ever carried out by the U.S.G.S. Part of the success of the expedition was due to the meticulous planning of Colonel Birdseye, the expedition leader. Colonel Birdseye was very careful about what could be brought and what had to be left behind, to the dismay of some members of the crew. The party of six scientific personnel, five boatmen, and a cook stayed in the Grand Canyon from the first of August to the first of October, recording many details about the Canyon. Studied and recorded were geology (for future damsites), depth of the

channel, speed of the current, and, as shown here, the flow of tributaries. Besides the Black Canyon damsite, twenty others were located and mapped within the Grand Canyon. Fortunately, and despite serious efforts in the 1960s, none of these dams were ever built.

Besides the scientific work of the survey, the party recorded a number of interesting firsts. They carried the first typewriter into the canyon as well as a large two-way radio to keep in touch with the outside world. The radio needed a 160-foot antenna to work, and despite warnings that it couldn't work in the deep canyons, work it did, so well that the crew often enjoyed listening to broadcasts in the evenings. Over the radio, they learned of the death of President Warren G. Harding. In his honor, they stayed in camp the day of his funeral and named the rapid opposite camp President Harding Rapid.

Portaging Hance Rapid, 1923

The 1923 Grand Canyon survey used five boats. Three were older boats owned by Southern California Edison that had been used on previous surveys, one was a brand new boat, and the last was a light, steel-framed canvas craft used to land the rodmen on ledges and in tight places in the canyon. The boats were named for canyons the survey would traverse: *Marble, Grand, Boulder, Glen,* and *Mojave.* For the bigger rapids, the boats were usually unloaded and the supplies and equipment carried along the shore. This arduous job could take whole days, and was earnestly hated by the boatmen. The passengers then walked around the rapids while the boatmen ran the lightened craft through the rapid. At only three places—Soap Creek, Lava Falls, and Separation Rapids—did they portage the boats as well. The boats used by the 1923 survey were not so forgiving as a modern inflatable raft. A hard knock on a rock would break a hole in the boat, necessitating sometimes lengthy repairs. Still, only one boat was lost. As the crew members were lining the *Mojave*, the light canvas boat, around Cave Springs rapid, the boat got away, was swept into the rocks, and destroyed. The other boatmen often lamented its loss in later days, when they had to maneuver the heavy wooden boats into a tiny cove to land a rodman. Supplies were replenished at certain points along the way by mule trains, as is shown in this photograph, by a crew led by LaRue's brother Roger. At Hance, the boatmen were able to use the supply mules to help in their portage of the rapid, easing their burden a great deal.

The Julian Steward Expedition at Lees Ferry, 1932

Julian Steward was a professor of anthropology at the University of Utah. He wanted to survey the archeological sites in Glen Canyon, which were most easily accessible by boat. So Steward rented two of Dave Rust's folding canoes and recruited a crew consisting of Charles Kelly, a western writer and explorer; Kelly's friend Hoffman Birney; Barney Hughes; and young Jack Shoemaker. The latter was the son of an eastern publisher who asked Steward to take young Jack on the trip to "make a man out of him." The party started from Hite, Utah, in July. The trip was plagued by windstorms which blew up clouds of sand, high water from recent rains which kept them from entering some of the side canyons Steward wanted to explore, and personality conflicts between Kelly and Birney, both experienced desert hands, and Steward, whom they considered a "dude." It was also, in Kelly's phrase, "hotternhell." Most of the sites along the river had long since been looted, and they didn't find much in the way of Indian artifacts. Despite the wind, the mud, the lack of success, and the conflicts, all in all they enjoyed their trip through the beautiful Glen Canyon. And, as Kelly later learned in a letter from the publisher, the trip was just what young Jack had needed.

Cal Tech Survey Party, plus Buzz Holmstrom, Lower Grand Canyon, 1937

Frank Dodge was by the 1930s considered to be one of the best boatmen ever to run the Colorado. Originally from Hawaii, he got his start on the Colorado with the Grand Canyon survey of 1923. Short, stocky, and very strong, he could swim like a seal and was afraid of "nothing wet." In 1937, he agreed to guide four scientists, two from the California Institute of Technology and two from the Pittsburgh Institute of Technology, through the Grand Canyon to study the ancient rock strata exposed in the innermost gorges. No expense was spared, nor was time a consideration. The party used expensive, mahogany-planked boats, and the latest in camping equipment on their two-month voyage. Later, one member of the party would comment that he was amazed at the way Dodge could control the boats and their crews by means of hand signals from the shore.

Near the end of their trip, they were overtaken by loner Haldane (Buzz) Holmstrom, who was on the home stretch of his 1,700-mile solo run of the Green and the Colorado. Holmstrom had originally applied to be one of the boatmen for the Cal Tech party, but when the position was filled he decided to go down the river with a friend. The friend thought better of the idea, however, and Buzz decided to go it alone. He met the Cal Tech scientists at Diamond Creek, stayed with them only for dinner, and went on to complete his run at Boulder Dam as he had started it, alone.

Trouble in the Canyon of Lodore, Utah Fish and Game Wildlife Survey, 1938

In the fall of 1938, Lee Kay of the Utah Department of Fish and Game conducted a search for bighorn sheep along the canyons and bottoms of the upper Green River. The once-plentiful sheep had disappeared from the rugged country around the river, and Kay was determined to find out why. He put together a crew consisting of Earl Clyde, a colleague from the Utah Fish and Game; Dr. Rasmussen, a biologist from Utah State University; Roy Despain; and Wes Eddington, a friend of Despain's. The party used two boats built by Despain, a vocational arts teacher from Springville, Utah. Despain had never built boats before, but he was a carpenter, and a good one. The boats turned out to be beauties; Lee Kay declared them to be the best boats ever used on the Green, and even Bus Hatch of Vernal, Utah, himself an experienced river hand and a good carpenter as well, was impressed by the quality. The

wildlife survey party left Hideout Flat, below Flaming Gorge, around the middle of September and reached Jensen about a month later. Dr. Kay concluded that the sheep had fallen victim to diseases introduced with domestic sheep. Four of the party, after they rescued their stranded boat shown in this photo, painted their names on the left-hand wall just below Triplet Falls, where they can still be seen. Roy Despain and Wes Eddington went on to run many more rivers in the next few decades.

University of Utah Ecological Survey Party in Glen Canyon, 1954

When the Bureau of Reclamation announced plans for a major dam in Glen Canyon, scientists of all kinds were quick to realize that this would be their last chance to study the many aspects of the canyon wildlife and plant community that would be covered by the rising waters of Lake Powell, as the new reservoir was to be called. One such scientist was a zoologist from the University of Utah, Dr. Angus Woodbury. Dr. Woodbury proposed to the Bureau that he be allowed to survey the ecological resources of the canyon and to accomplish that end, took several trips through Glen Canyon in the 1950s. These trips, as well as studies of other reservoir sites in surrounding states, resulted in a dozen scientific publications on birds, plant communities, and environment of areas now lost forever. In the boat with Dr. Woodbury in this photo are Dr. Walter Cottam, an internationally known botanist from the University of Utah; Dr. Albert Grundmann, zoologist; and Dr. Herbert Riesbol, biologist. Driving the boat is Jack Brennan, a long-time river outfitter who gave up his half of Harris-Brennan River Expeditions to work full time guiding similar parties through Glen Canyon as the dam was being built.

Bureau of Reclamation Surveyor, Glen Canyon Damsite, 1956

Construction work on the Glen Canyon Dam began soon after Congress authorized the Colorado River Storage Project in 1954. In many ways, this was a culmination of over fifty years of efforts by engineers and hydrologists to place a dam in Glen Canyon. E. C. LaRue, for instance, had ruined his career with the U.S.G.S. through his dogged and sometimes bitter support of just such a dam. LaRue had wanted a dam only a mile above Lees Ferry, but the site finally chosen was about fifteen miles above that. The choice of Glen Canyon at all was another compromise, in part to resolve a controversy over the proposed Echo Park Dam on the Green River in Dinosaur National Monument. The Bureau had intended to someday build a dam in Glen Canyon as part of the Colorado River Storage Project, but when the Echo Park Dam was defeated in Congress, planning for the Glen Canyon Dam was speeded up. Ironically, Glen Canyon was part of the Escalante National Monument that was proposed in 1938. Inclusion in the National Parks system would have precluded building the Glen Canyon Dam, but the proposed monument was violently opposed by ranching and mining interests in Utah and the proclamation was never signed. Here a Bureau of Reclamation crew seeks relief from the relentless desert sun.

Dr. C. Gregory Crampton in Glen Canyon

Dr. Crampton was a member of the history faculty at the University of Utah when the decision to build Glen Canyon Dam was announced. Plans for an archaeological salvage survey were already in place, under the direction of Dr. Jesse Jennings, archaeologist from the University of Utah, but there was no provision to salvage the history of the canyon. Dr. Crampton realized, from his long-time study of the history of the area, that the rich historical heritage in Glen Canyon should also be preserved. He took his idea for an extensive survey to the National Park Service and Dr. Jennings; when asked if he had anyone in mind who was qualified to conduct such a study, Dr. Crampton replied that he knew someone who was very well qualified indeed. Dr. Crampton and his students spent six years in Glen Canyon and the lower San Juan River canyon, locating, surveying, photographing, and recording every possible historic site that was to be covered by the waters of Lake Powell. They studied everything from mining camps to historic inscriptions to abandoned steamboats to steps cut into the walls by forgotten miners. Out of his researches came at least half-a-dozen publications, including *The Outline History of Glen Canyon, 1776–1922, The Hoskaninni Mining Papers: Mining in Glen Canyon, 1897–1902,* and many others. Dr. Crampton's interest in the river and the canyons has continued for the rest of his life and resulted in many more works on the region.

CHAPTER 2
Prospectors

After two years of hard work of exploration of the Colorado and its tributaries, I find myself penniless and disgusted with the whole thing, sitting under a Mesquite bush in the sand. I write this journal hoping that it will give a faint idea of the country at large. If anybody disbelieves any of this or wants to know more of the cañons of the Colorado—go and see it. Before we started I was called a damned fool for embarking in such an enterprise, for nobody possibly gets through. Since I have got through, I have been called a damned fool for the same thing . . .

—Jack Sumner, Journal, 1869

The California gold rush created the state of mind that led to later rushes along the Colorado River and its tributaries. Much of the gold found in California had come from the beds of mountains streams, extracted by means of sluice boxes. If there was a little gold in a mountain stream, so the typical American reasoning went, there must be a lot of gold in a big river—the Colorado—which was fed by those streams. Thus was born the concept of "nature's sluice box," the idea that all the gold washed out of the Rocky Mountains would eventually make its way to the Colorado River.

Theodore Hook of Cheyenne, Wyoming, was one of the first prospectors to follow this line of reasoning. In May 1869, just a few days after John Wesley Powell left Green River, Wyoming, Hook followed him with a group of miners. The prospectors made it only as far as Red Canyon, however, before their boat overturned and Hook drowned.

Others soon followed; it was the lure of mineral wealth that led James White to the San Juan River, where he and his friends were ambushed by Indians. Only White survived, reportedly by making a raft and floating all the way through the Grand Canyon. Also in the Grand Canyon, discoveries of small gold and silver deposits at the mouth of Kanab Creek set off a periodic mining boom that lasted until the 1890s, when a copper boom flared up. Captain John Hance, William Bass, and many others were lured to the Grand Canyon by the prospects for mineral wealth there, and some actually made money at it. Grand Canyon was too big and too hard to get in and out of, however, so many miners focused on Glen Canyon.

In 1880, two prospectors named Mitchell and Merrick reportedly found a fabulous silver mine in the Navajo lands south of Glen Canyon. Before they could exploit the lode, they were killed by Indians in Monument Valley (where two buttes are named for them), and the secret of the mine's location was lost. As the legend of the Lost Mine of Pish-la-ki (Navajo for silver) grew, prospectors flocked into the Glen Canyon region. One of the first was Cass Hite, whose persistent search for the Mitchell and Merrick mine earned him the name "Hosteen Pish-la-ki"—Mr. Silver Hunter—from the Navajos. After a few years of fruitless search for the lost mine, Hite was asked by Hoskanini, the Navajo chief, why he was looking for silver when there was gold in the sands of the river? Hite followed the chief's advice, and sure enough, found gold in Glen Canyon. When word of his discovery got out, the idea of "nature's sluice box" took hold. Prospectors came to the region by the hundreds, and before long there was hardly a wide place along the river without at least one mining claim staked on it.

By far the biggest operation in Glen Canyon was the Hoskaninni Mining Company, a product of the imagination and boundless energies of Robert Brewster Stanton. Undaunted by the disastrous failure of the Denver, Colorado Canyon and Pacific Railroad a decade before and convinced that the so-called flour gold could be recovered, Stanton persuaded a number of wealthy industrialists to finance the company. Despite Stanton's best efforts, however, which included the building of a giant floating dredge, running a telephone line, and many other improvements, the gold proved impossible to recover and the company was bankrupt by 1902. Less than ten years later, another energetic visionary tried again to recover the elusive flour gold. Charles H. Spencer put fully as much time and effort into his workings at Lees Ferry as had Stanton, but was no more successful. The efforts of the American Placer Company, Spencer's backer, marked the high tide of mining along the river, even though sporadic efforts continued in Glen Canyon until it was flooded by Lake Powell.

A similar boom-bust cycle was occurring along the San Juan River at about the same time. Rumors of gold along the San Juan had been in circulation since a man named Goodridge had floated the river on a prospecting trip in 1883. It wasn't until a decade later, however, that a real rush developed. In the autumn of 1892, newspapers in Utah and Colorado were suddenly full of stories of rich strikes along the lower San Juan. Where the stories came from no one knew, but there was little truth to them, as many miners who came to the region soon found to their disgust. Reportedly, one disgruntled miner offered a reward of $100 for the "fool who started this rush."

There *was* gold in the San Juan canyon; Walter Mendenhall reportedly recovered $4,000 worth in 1894 and 1895, and Bert Loper told how he had recovered more than twenty ounces himself. But like most rushes, those who found gold and made money were far outnumbered by those who tried and failed. Among the latter was Charles Spencer. Before moving to Lees Ferry to try his luck there, Spencer had had a large operation on the San Juan river. Although thousands of dollars were poured into the development, little or no gold was recovered.

The twentieth century heralded the arrival of

the automobile and gasoline engines, and consequently an increased demand for oil. In the first decades of the century a number of oil booms flared to life and just as quickly died away. The first of these was along the San Juan. When Goodridge floated the river back in 1883, he noted oil seeps at many points along the river, and had drilled a number of wells. A gusher at Mexican Hat started a rush that brought, among others, William E. Nevills, father of Norman Nevills. The difficulties of transportation in and out of the rugged and remote canyon of the San Juan, however, coupled with the lack of refining facilities, precluded any real development until the Aneth field was opened farther upstream in the 1950s. The same problem retarded development of oil wells drilled along the Colorado below Moab in the 1920s, all of which could only be supplied by boat. When one of the wells burned in a spectacular fire in 1925, drilling along the river was abandoned and never resumed.

The final great rush for riches occurred in the late 1940s and early 1950s. A demand by the U.S. government for uranium to feed its expanding nuclear arsenal set off a rush that approached madness in the lands around the Green, Colorado, and San Juan. Mining claims were staked and filed by the thousands, and millions of shares of stock in new mining companies—most of it worthless—were traded back and forth by eager investors. When the government announced that it had enough uranium, the boom collapsed and the rivers were once again left in peace.

There were other rushes and other developments—coal in Desolation Canyon, copper along the upper Green, potash on the Colorado near Moab, even asbestos and bat guano in the Grand Canyon. Some were successful and some were not. With a few notable exceptions very little wealth was ever extracted from mines or wells along the rivers for the simple reason that the river canyons were too hard to get to, and more than that, much too difficult to get ore out of. Nature guarded her sluice box very well indeed.

John C. Sumner in Glen Canyon, 1897

Jack Sumner was operating a trading post in Middle Park, Colorado, in 1867, when he was approached by Major John Wesley Powell and asked to join an expedition to explore the Green and Colorado rivers. Sumner jumped at the chance, and during the 1869 expedition, was one of the outstanding men in the crew. Sumner was entrusted with the Major's boat, and on a number of occasions risked his own life to save others, including, on at least one occasion, Powell himself. Despite this, and despite promises made by Powell at the start of the trip, when the party emerged from the Grand Canyon at the end of August 1869, Powell and his brother essentially abandoned the remaining crew members and traveled back to Washington, D.C., to the accolades of the nation. Sumner, like the others, found himself penniless and far from home.

In 1871, when Powell was planning his second exploring voyage, Sumner was the only member of the first crew who he asked to be on the second. Unfortunately, late spring snows delayed Sumner as he traveled to the rendezvous and Powell was forced to leave without him. In 1873, Sumner was married in Iowa, but soon returned to the country around the Colorado River, where he lived the rest of his life. When Robert Brewster Stanton was passing through Glen Canyon in 1889, he spied a bearded man sitting on the river bank. Stopping to talk, Stanton discovered the man was none other than Jack Sumner, who was prospecting in the nearby Henry Mountains. Stanton questioned Sumner closely about the rapids and dangers to come, and after returning home began a correspondence with Sumner that lasted until the latter's death in 1907. Thanks to Stanton, Sumner wrote out a full, if belated, account of his experiences with John Wesley Powell, which was later published in *Colorado River Controversies*, a much-edited version of Stanton's massive history of the Colorado River.

Cass Hite at Ticaboo, Glen Canyon 1907

Cass Hite was one of the first prospectors to enter the Glen Canyon region, arriving in September 1883. After being advised by the Navajo chief Hoskanini to look for gold in the sandbars along the river bottoms, Hite prospected down the river from the mouth of White

Canyon. There he did indeed find gold, but more important, he found a home. Hite was thirty-eight years old when he moved to the ford at the head of Glen Canyon. He started a ferry at that place, sometimes called "Dandy Crossing" because it was such a dandy place to cross the river. Hite prospected, farmed, took the occasional traveler across the river, and built several cabins near the ferry—since called Hite—or at nearby Ticaboo. In 1891, Hite got in a gunfight in Green River, Utah, and killed his opponent. Even though the other man fired first, Hite was found guilty of murder and sentenced to twelve years in prison. He spent just over a year in the Utah State Penitentiary in Salt Lake City before contracting tuberculosis. Through the efforts of his brother, John Hite, he was pardoned by Governor Caleb West so he could go home to die. Hite was nursed back to health by friends in Hanksville, Utah, and returned to his home on the Colorado. Hite lived through boom and bust, and saw engineers, miners, and prospectors come and go. He finally died as he had lived, alone, in 1914 at his ranch on Ticaboo Creek. He was found by Alonzo G. Turner and was buried by his brother, John, and his friend and neighbor Bert Loper in the canyon that had been his home for so many years.

William Bass in His Cable Car, at the Foot of the Bass Trail

William Wallace Bass was from Indiana, and came to the Grand Canyon for his health in 1883. He tried his hand at mining, but soon realized that there was more money to be made (for less effort!) by guiding the increasing numbers of tourists who came to see the Grand Canyon. Between 1885 and 1901, Bass built more than fifty miles of trails in the canyon to bring guests to Bass Camp, his resort on the north side of the river. There he had tent cabins, corrals, and a small garden and orchard watered by Shinumo Creek. To get across the river Bass strung a cable with a car; many nervous passengers must have wondered, during the hair-raising crossing in a swinging cable car, if Bass Camp was worth the ride above the swirling waters of the muddy Colorado. When an eastern tourist, Ada Diefendorf, visited the canyon in 1892, she fell in love with William and they were soon married; this union produced the first white children born at the Grand Canyon. Besides his tourist business, Bass drove a stage from Williams, Arizona, to the South Rim and the El Tovar Lodge. A sensitive and artistic man, Bass wrote poetry about the wonders of the canyon, played the vio-

lin, and kept notebooks with his philosophical musings about the origins of the river and the canyon. When Bass died in 1933, his ashes were scattered across Holy Grail Temple, now called Bass Tomb.

Start of the Best Expedition, Green River, Utah, July 12, 1891

Harry McDonald was a boatman with the Stanton railroad survey in 1890, and had been excited by the prospects he saw in the granite at the bottom of the Grand Canyon. Stanton, however, refused to allow him to stake a claim. McDonald, in a huff, quit the party then and there and made an epic solo winter climb to the North Rim of the Grand Canyon. He made his way to Denver, where he looked up a mining speculator named James Best. Inspired by McDonald's description, Best formed the Colorado and Grand Canyon Mining and Improvement Company. McDonald told Best and his partners that the prospects were rich and unclaimed, but—perhaps remembering his experience climbing out—insisted that they could only be reached by boat. Best ordered two boats of the same design as those used by Stanton, organized a crew, and amid the usual fanfare of those days left Green River in July. The 120 miles of Labyrinth and Stillwater canyons were easy, but twelve miles into Cataract Canyon one of the boats was smashed against a rock and lost. This inspired one of the forlorn crew to scratch a picture of a sinking boat on a nearby boulder with the bitter inscription: "Hell to Pay. No. 1 sunk and down." Disillusioned, the party continued on to Hite in the remaining boat, borrowed a skiff, and floated on to Lees Ferry. There the remaining boat and the mining venture were promptly abandoned.

Williams-Cahn Placer Mining Barge on the San Juan River, Mouth of Copper Canyon, 1894

J. P. Williams was one of the organizers of the Gabel Mining District, which included the San Juan below Clay Hills Crossing. During the gold rush to the San Juan region in the winter of 1892, prospectors set up numerous mining districts and the area was blanketed with claims. Copper Canyon was one of the few places along the San Juan below Bluff, Utah, where the river could be reached by road; as a consequence it was the scene of more activity than most places in the canyon. The boiler and other equipment on this barge was probably freighted in from a railroad station in Colorado, over 150 miles away. A placer is a gravel or sand bar along the river, which often contains gold. The boiler in this photo was probably

used to run a pump; the stream of water from the pump would loosen the gravel and sand in the placer, which was then directed into a sluice box. The sluice was run over plates coated with mercury. The heavier gold sank to the bottom and bonded with the mercury while the sand and gravel washed on out. The mercury was then boiled off to obtain the gold. However, for all their efforts, very few miners ever struck it rich in the San Juan canyon.

Bert Loper in the Canyon of Lodore, 1922

Albert Loper was born in 1869, the same year that Major Powell made his pioneering voyage down the Green and Colorado. It is fitting that Loper should have come into the world that very year, for by the time of his death eighty years later, Loper would be known as "the Grand Old Man of the Colorado." Loper first came to the river during the gold rush to the San Juan canyons in the early 1890s and stayed around the Colorado for the rest of his life. He was familiar with the canyons of the Green River, those on the upper Colorado such as Westwater, Cataract, and Glen Canyon, and the San Juan canyons, but by the time he neared his seventieth birthday in 1939, had never been through the Grand Canyon. That winter, he was in the hospital recovering from an operation, when he had a visitor. Young Don Harris had been a boatman for Nevills' expedition the year before, and now wanted to go down the Grand Canyon. He came to the Grand Old Man of the Colorado for advice. Bert gave him more than that; the next summer, when Harris was ready to go, Loper was recovered and rowing one of two boats. They had a grand trip, and at the end of the canyon, just before Bert turned seventy, they decided to repeat it in ten years when he turned eighty. No one but Bert took the idea seriously, but he did, and in July 1949 was at Lees Ferry with a new boat and a fresh determination. Bert had recently had heart trouble and was not well; at one point he told the others—who included Harris but no one else who had been on the 1939 trip—that if anything happened he wanted to be buried in the canyon. A few days into the canyon, as they approached the rapid at mile 24.5, Bert refused to stop and scout it, saying he was too tired. The boat, with Wayne Nichols as passenger, entered the rapid and suddenly went out of control and overturned. Nichols caught onto the lifeline of the boat and saw Bert, floating through the rapid, his eyes open, apparently dead or dying. Nichols couldn't hold onto Bert's boat, and it too soon went downstream. The others soon caught up and the desolate party began their grim search for Bert. At the mouth of Buck Farm Canyon, sixteen miles downstream from where it had gotten away, they found not Bert but his boat. Since it was obvious by now that Bert was gone, they pulled the boat up above high water and wrote his epitaph on the front deck: "Bert Loper, Grand Old Man of the Colorado, Born: July 31, 1869. Died: July 8, 1949." Bert's wife, Rachel, grieved for Bert for the next twenty-five years until she died in February 1975. Just two months later, a hiker found a skeleton at the mouth of Cardeñas Creek, almost fifty miles from where Bert had run his last rapid. Forensic analysis showed that the bones were indeed those of Bert Loper, who was taken from his beloved canyons and buried next to his wife in Sandy, Utah. Just as it was fitting that Loper should be born when river running on the Colorado got its start, it was equally fitting that he should die at the dawn of the era of commercial river travel.

Robert Brewster Stanton in Glen Canyon, 1897

Stanton was one of the most interesting figures in the history of the Colorado River. He first came to the river in 1889 as chief engineer of an ill-fated survey for the Denver, Colorado Canyon, and Pacific Railway Co. By the time this picture was taken, Stanton was back on the Colorado as engineer for the Hoskaninni Mining Company in Glen Canyon. Stanton envisioned mining the placer bars along the river for the "flour gold" they were known to contain and organized the company in 1897. Again, Stanton devoted his considerable energies and talents to the project, but again it was a failure. Unable to stay away from the river, Stanton turned to collecting the history and lore of the Colorado, seeking out survivors of the Powell expeditions and digging through archives all over the country. He produced a 1,200 page manuscript called *The River and the Canyon*, but was unable to find a publisher before he died in 1922. In all other things he was a success, but when it came to the Colorado, Stanton failed and failed big.

Freighters on the San Juan Near Bluff, 1900

These five unidentified prospectors were on their way down to an isolated mining camp in the canyon of the San Juan. Since the deep, incised canyons were all but inaccessible by land, supplies and equipment had to be floated down the river on barges and boats to the mining claims, most of which were on the lower San Juan, below Clay Hills Crossing. Supplies consisted of nonperishable goods since there was no refrigeration: beans, flour, coffee (such as the box of Arbuckles coffee visible in the boat on the left), dried beef, bacon, some canned foods. Perhaps a bottle of whiskey or two was included to pass the time in the lonely camp. It was on just such a venture that riverman Norman Nevills got his start. Nevills moved to the small town of Mexican Hat in 1925, when he was nineteen years old. A few years later, a local man had a job hauling supplies downriver to a mining camp in the canyon of the San Juan backed out at the last moment, fearing the legends that the Navajos told of the mad, dangerous river were true after all. But the miners had to have their supplies; young Norman was asked if he would take the boat down. He did, successfully, and the rest is history.

Nathaniel Galloway in Glen Canyon, Around 1900

Nathaniel Galloway, or "Than," as his friends called him, was a prospector, trapper, and sometimes orchard keeper who lived in Vernal, Utah. More than for any of these occupations, he is known today as the premier riverman of his time. Before Galloway began running rivers in the 1880s, river voyagers used rowboats in the manner standard for centuries: they rowed with their backs to the direction of travel, either looking over their shoulders or depending on a steersman for direction. Consequently, the boats had to be sturdy so they could (hopefully!) withstand continuous crashing into rocks in the rapids or, more frequently, being dragged along the shore. Most early expeditions avoided running rapids altogether, preferring to portage or line their boats around the falls, much to the disgust of the crewmen. Galloway was the first river runner to apply the principle of facing the danger, and the first to run rapids confidently instead of walking around them. Contrary to the accepted practice of the time, he faced his boat downstream in a rapid and used the oars to position himself for the best run. By slowing the boat with the oars, he could maneuver through the rapid and avoid crashing into rocks or falling into "holes" where the boat could be capsized or caught. Galloway also designed his own boats, which were light skiffs about

fourteen-feet long, flat-bottomed, and with a pronounced rake or curve fore and aft. The Galloway boat became the standard river craft until the advent of inflatable rafts at the end of World War II. Galloway was such a skilled oarsman that a friend once remarked that all he needed to successfully run a boat was "a heavy dew."

Assessment Work in Glen Canyon, 1900

The Hoskaninni Mining Company came about as a result of the efforts of that remarkable and energetic man, Robert Brewster Stanton. After the failure of the Denver, Colorado Canyon, and Pacific Railway Co. in 1890, Stanton turned to other engineering pursuits to rebuild his fortunes. But he never forgot the Colorado River; more specifically, he never forgot the gold he had seen in the placer bars in Glen Canyon. He had, in fact, staked several claims while the railroad survey crews were struggling through the shallow waters of Glen Canyon. Convinced that the gold could be recovered, Stanton persuaded two wealthy industrialists, Julius Stone and Frank S. Brooks, that mining the placer bars could be profitable if it was just done right. With their backing, Stanton organized the Hoskaninni Mining Company in 1897. He and his crews staked and filed claims on virtually the entire length of Glen Canyon. Once a mining claim is made, however, the law requires that a certain amount of "assessment work" be done to keep the claim valid year to year. Crews from the Hoskaninni Mining Co. improved old trails and roads, constructed new ones, strung a telephone line, and built several camps in the canyon, two of which they named Camp Stone and Camp Brooks in honor of the investors—Camp Stone alone had over seventy-five men working in it at one time. Their biggest, and most futile effort, however, was the giant floating dredge they built at river's edge in 1900. The placer gold proved to be too fine to recover after all, and the company went under. It was bankrupt by 1902, and the entire assets of the company—camps, roads, buildings, dredge—were bought at a tax auction by a man from Salt Lake City for $200.

The Remains of the Hoskaninni Mining Company Dredge, Glen Canyon, 1938

The Hoskaninni Mining Co. dredge was built by the Bucyrus Co. of South Milwaukee, Wisconsin. (Its successor, Bucyrus-Erie, still makes giant earthmoving equipment today). The dredge was built at the Bucyrus plant, disassembled and shipped by rail to Green River, Utah. It was then hauled by freight wagons across one hundred miles of desert to Glen Canyon. The dredge was reassembled at Camp Wilson, launched there, then moved upriver to Camp Stone, where it was put to work in March 1901. The dredge alone cost over $100,000. When complete, it was the largest machine ever to operate in Glen Canyon—105 feet long, 36 feet wide, and 2 stories tall. The business end consisted of forty-six three-cubic-yard buckets, powered by five separate gasoline engines. It must have been an impressive sight in operation: the great rattling chain of buckets bringing up a constant stream of primordial sand and mud from the river bottom, the gasoline engines roaring. But things went wrong from the outset. The shifting river bottom, the changes in the water level, and problems with the gold recovery apparatus plagued Stanton from the start. After two months of operation, the total value of gold recovered by the dredge was $66.95. When the company went into receivership in 1902, the new owners of the dredge moved it and tried again, but the results were the same; and finally the dredge was tied up to the riverbank and left to decay. Successive floods moved and finally smashed the huge structure, and by the time it was covered by Lake Powell, it was nothing but a jumble of timber and rusting iron.

Charles H. Spencer at Lees Ferry, 1910

"Charles H. Spencer is an enigma in the history of the canyons," wrote western historians Rusho and Crampton in their book on Lees Ferry, *Desert River Crossing*. "Although he pursued the quest for gold, he seemed to enjoy the pursuit more than the gold." Spencer was a self-taught mining engineer who held experts in low contempt. His first try at the elusive gold in the canyon country was Spencer's Camp on the San Juan, 125 miles upriver from Lees Ferry, where he tried for a year to extract the gold in the Wingate sandstone. When that failed, he moved to Lees Ferry and set his sights on the Chinle formation, a loosely bedded shale lying below the Wingate. The Chinle was exposed at Lees Ferry, and there were supplies of coal nearby which could run boilers, and hence pumps to blast the rock loose. With the backing of the American Placer Company, Spencer started operations at Lees Ferry in 1910. This was a much more impressive operation than Spencer's Camp. There were several boilers which powered pumps, called monitors, shooting high-pressure jets of river water. Spencer also built many buildings (mostly torn down by the Park Service in the 1960s) to house his large crew of workmen, who were busy mining, building trails, and maintaining the equipment. The latter included a flotilla of river craft, such as a powered launch and a ninety-two-foot steamboat. Despite all his preparations and efforts, however, Spencer's dream proved as elusive as Stanton's, and the operation folded after only a few months. The major problem

was the gold recovery apparatus, which kept clogging with an unknown element. Ironically, it turned out that the unknown element was rhenium, today a highly valued metal used as a superconductor of electricity.

The Steamboat *Charles H. Spencer* in Glen Canyon, 1911
The Wreck of the *Charles H. Spencer,* Lees Ferry, 1985

The *Charles H. Spencer* was the brainchild of Dr. Julius Koebig, an official of the American Placer Co. Except for the Hoskaninni dredge, it was the largest craft ever to float in Glen Canyon. The steamboat was ninety-two feet long, with a beam of twenty-five feet, powered by a twelve-foot paddle wheel at the stern. It was built in San Francisco in 1911, dismantled, and shipped to Marysvale, Utah, by rail. From there, the boat was hauled two hundred miles to Glen Canyon, reassembled, launched, and named, over Spencer's objections, after him. The purpose of this grand craft was to haul coal from mines at Warm Creek to Lees

Ferry to power the boilers, mills, and pumps of Spencer's gold-mining operation. After some difficulty finding a crew among the miners, cowboys, prospectors, and hangers-on around Lees Ferry, the captain, Pete Hanna (far left in the photograph) took it on its maiden voyage in 1912. This started inauspiciously when the boat hung on a sandbar a hundred yards from its launch. Once the crew got it refloated, they learned that it took as much coal as the boat could carry just to make the run from Lees Ferry to the coal mine at Warm Creek. Captain Pete Hanna soon figured out a way to haul the needed coal on a barge, however, and it looked like the big paddle-wheeler would soon be making regular runs in Glen Canyon. Before a regular run could be established, however, Spencer's grand scheme had gone bust. The *Charles H. Spencer* was tied up just below the ferry landing at Lees Ferry and left to the river. In 1915, a major flood on the Colorado forced a raft of driftwood up under the boat; when the high water subsided, the unbalanced boat tipped on its side and sank in shallow water. At some later date the superstructure was salvaged for the timber, but the massive hull and boilers were too large to move, and they were left where the boat sank. They are still visible, especially in today's clear water, just a hundred yards or so above the modern Lees Ferry boat ramp. The wreck of the *Charles H. Spencer* is one of the few reminders of the hectic boom days in Glen Canyon.

Charles Smith in Cataract Canyon, October 1911

Before the gates on Glen Canyon Dam were closed in 1963, Cataract Canyon comprised forty miles of some of the most ferocious whitewater in North America. The river fell over 425 feet in that distance, an average of over ten feet per mile (by contrast, the Mississippi falls only inches per mile). Major Powell had taken twelve days to traverse it in 1869, and so many prospectors had disappeared trying to get to Glen Canyon that Cataract had earned the reputation of the "Graveyard of the Colorado." The worst rapid was reputedly one of the last before Hite, Dark Canyon Rapid. Dark Canyon was a long rocky fall with a sharp bend at the end and a rocky island in the middle. Dark Canyon Rapid and indeed all but eleven miles of Cataract's rapids were covered by Lake Powell as it filled.

In October 1911, as the Kolb brothers were working their way through Cataract, they ran into a prospector named Charles E. W. Smith in an old, leaky boat. Ellsworth Kolb described him as "about medium size, but . . . tough and wiry. He had lost one eye, the other was that light gray color that is usually associated with indomitable nerve. He . . . gave the impression of being very capable." Indeed, Smith's main worry when the brothers met him seemed to be that his tobacco had spoiled. When the Kolbs warned him of the dangerous rapids ahead and offered to let him accompany them the rest of the way through, Smith smiled and replied "I guess there will be some way through." Smith did make it that time, as well as another trip the next year. But in November 1913, he left his home in Green River on a trapping trip, and was never seen again. John Hite and Bert Loper found his wrecked boat in Cataract Canyon the next year.

Rivermen on the *Undine*, Early 1900s

Powered boats on the Green and Colorado were tried almost as soon as the towns of Moab and Green River were founded. The first steamboat, the MAJOR POWELL, was on the water as early as 1891, although it took another ten years of effort before the first powered craft, the *Undine*, made the 360-mile round trip between the two towns. The *Undine* was lost upriver from Moab shortly afterwards, but by the time that happened, a number of enterprising individuals had built and operated steam- or gasoline-powered boats, launches, and scows. The craft were used to haul everything from men, machinery, and supplies to remote mining claims, speculators to a proposed resort hotel, even fruit from Moab to the railroad in Green River. There was Cap Yokey (far right), of Green River, who built the *Black Eagle*, a side-wheeler that worked fine until it exploded in 1907; Edwin Wolverton (second from right), the first successful steamboat man, who built the *Wilmont* in 1903, followed by the *Navajo* a few years later; Milton Oppenheimer, who ran the *Paddy Ross* up and down the river for a decade; H. Elwyn Blake, Sr., who planned to ship fruit from orchards in Moab and whose son became a renowned riverman in his own right; and Tom Wimmer, who was up and down the river from his ranch at the mouth of the San Rafael from 1906 to 1925. Also in this photograph is Ross Wheeler (far left), a friend of Bert Loper's. After Wheeler was

killed in a barroom fight, Loper named his next boat after him. Later, the boat was abandoned in the Grand Canyon, and can still be seen near the foot of the Bass Trail. These and other resourceful men made the remote canyons of the Green and Colorado into lively places for almost four decades.

Moab Garage Co. Launch on the Colorado Below Moab, 1924

People, supplies, and freight weren't the only things hauled on the Colorado during the oil boom of the 1920s. In this photograph, two horses are being transported in one of the powered launches operated by the Moab Garage and Transportation Co. Clarence, Virgil, and Dennis Baldwin ran a small fleet of boats, barges, launches, and scows on the Colorado below Moab and the confluence with the Green, some sixty miles one way, for years. The brothers hauled passengers and freight to a series of oil wells that were drilled downstream from Moab during a boom that lasted from 1924 until 1929. During that period they made almost 250 round trips of eighty miles each, using a variety of craft, including one of the largest to operate on the Colorado, a seventy-five-foot scow powered by a Ford car engine. Virgil Baldwin later remembered that the river was always too low or too high: "At first the water in the river was low for boating and then about the 15th of May, to the same time in June, almost too high to be safe." But those who supply booms always do better than the boomers, and so it was with the Baldwin brothers. The oil boom came to nothing after a promising gusher was killed when an overzealous oil engineer pumped tons of drilling mud down the drill hole to stop the uncontrolled flow, but the Baldwins continued hauling whatever was needed down the river for many years.

Japanese Placer Miners at the Mouth of Hansen Creek, Glen Canyon, July 1938

Despite the fact that a generation of prospectors had tried to extract gold from the sands of Glen Canyon and despite the experiences of engineers such as Robert Brewster Stanton with his big expensive placer-mining dredge, the lure of color glinting in the sandbars still drew prospectors. When Norm Nevills was passing through Glen Canyon on his 1938 river expedition, he noticed recent workings at what was known as Smith Bar, below the mouth of Hansen Creek. The diggings at Smith Bar were some of the oldest in the canyon, having been worked off and on since 1888. Nevills had heard of some Japanese miners and hoped to meet them; sure enough, just below their claim he saw them standing on the riverbank motioning, so he landed. Their names were Homma, Kameda, and Tom Inouye, and they had driven an old pickup truck down Hansen Creek to get to their claims. What dreams of riches could have lured this improbable trio so far and to such a remote place? Due to the language barrier, Nevills could learn little of how they were faring, but he did note that theirs was the neatest and cleanest mining camp he had ever seen.

CHAPTER 3
Photographers

[T]he success of our expedition depended on our success as photographers. We could not hope to add anything of importance to the scientific and topographic knowledge of the canyons already existing; and merely to come out alive at the other end did not make a strong appeal to our vanity. We were there as scenic photographers in love with their work, and determined to reproduce the marvels of the Colorado's canyons, as far as we could do it. . . . We had no real assurance that so delicate an apparatus [a motion picture camera], always difficult to use and regulate, could even survive the journey—much less, in such inexperienced hands as ours, reproduce its wonders. But this, nevertheless, was our secret hope, hardly admitted to our most intimate friends—that we could bring out a record of the Colorado as it is, a live thing, armed as it were with teeth, ready to crush and devour.

—Ellsworth Kolb, *Through the Grand Canyon from Wyoming to Mexico*, 1914

The earliest photographers to record the wonders of the canyons of the Green and Colorado were members of various scientific surveys that crisscrossed the West in the 1870s. Earlier surveys to penetrate the river canyons, such as Ives' in 1857–58, had had to rely on artists for visual impressions. Many times the enormity of the landscape, so outside the realm of experience up to that time, resulted in impressionistic works that make the Grand Canyon resemble Dante's inferno more than the canyon of the Colorado River. One of the problems was with the cameras in use at the time. Called wet-plate photography, the taking of images required a heavy and awkward camera box, fragile glass plates, containers of various kinds of chemicals to fix the image, and a darkroom.

The demands of taking pictures during the Civil War, however, caused photographers to refine the process enough that by the end of the conflict, field photography was a well-practiced art. A photographer in the field still required a whole wagon (or boat, in Powell's case) to carry camera, plates, chemicals, and a portable darkroom, but at least it was now possible. The first photographer to see the bottoms of the canyons was E. O. Beaman, who floated the Green and the Colorado with John Wesley Powell in 1871. Beaman, an experienced photographer from New York, took many fine views, but did not get along with the irascible Major Powell. When the expeditions established winter quarters at Kanab, Utah, in 1871, Beaman resigned and returned home to New York and published his photos, trying to beat Powell into print. His eventual replacement was another member of the expedition, John K. Hillers, who had no training in photography, but soon proved to have a natural talent for taking pictures. Another government photographer of the time was Timothy O'Sullivan, who was attached to Lt. George Wheeler's Geographical Survey West of the 100th Meridian. O'Sullivan recorded Wheeler's ascent into the lower Grand Canyon in 1871.

Franklin A. Nims, a photographer from Colorado Springs, Colorado, was hired to document the ill-fated survey of the Colorado River by the Denver, Colorado Canyon, and Pacific Railway Company in 1889. Nims survived all of the disasters which befell the survey party, only to be incapacitated by a fall from a cliff on New Year's Day 1890. After Nims was injured, Robert Brewster Stanton took over the camera—by this time, film cameras had replaced wet plates—and completed the photographic record of the survey.

In the first decades of the twentieth century, a number of men simultaneously got the idea of photographing the canyons and then selling the pictures to newspapers or magazines. Among the first, and certainly the least successful, was Charles Silver Russell, a mining promoter and erstwhile newspaperman. Russell took two trips down the Colorado, in 1907 and again in 1914, for the purpose of making marketable pictures of a run down the river. Both trips were remarkably unsuccessful. Each time Russell lost cameras, film, boats. After the second, Russell gave up the river and returned to mining; later he went insane and had to be committed to an institution.

A much more successful photographer was Raymond Cogswell, who accompanied Julius Stone on his trip down the Green and the Colorado in 1909. Cogswell took over 2,000 fine images and kept detailed notes on lighting conditions, colors, and locations. Stone, however, was a millionaire and not really interesting in selling the pictures. It wasn't until 1932 that a fraction of the photos Cogswell took appeared in Stone's book, *Canyon Country*. Two years after Stone's voyage, the Kolb brothers, Ellsworth and Emery, successfully tapped the market for pictures of the Colorado and its canyons. They floated the Green and the Colorado in 1911 and on the way made the most complete photographic record of the river up to that time. They also did something new; they made the first motion pictures of running rapids. Many of their photos were displayed in their studio on the South Rim of the Grand Canyon, and the film made on their trip was shown practically every day until Emery's death in 1976.

During the U.S. government surveys of the river canyons in the 1920s, photographers took literally thousands of pictures of damsites, geological formations, and other places of likely bureaucratic interest. Many of the pictures were taken by government surveyors, but some were taken by the Kolb brothers, who served on several of the trips.

In 1927 Clyde Eddy, a combat veteran of World War I and an employee of a large pharmaceutical firm, decided to float the Colorado River and make a film of the trip. Interest in the river was keen, due to the recent announcement of government plans to build a high dam in Black Canyon on the lower Colorado. Eddy secured a newsreel cameraman to fill the expedition, but the cameraman lasted only as far as Lees Ferry before abandoning the river. In the end, Eddy was left with only an incomplete film and still photographs to document the trip.

Eddy had been spurred in his decision to float the river by the announcement that the Pathe-Bray Company had been formed to produce a feature film about running the Colorado River. The film, variously titled *Bride of the Colorado* and *Pride of the Colorado*, was to be a standard action yarn of the times, set in Cataract and Grand Canyons. Much footage was shot and much hardship endured by cast and crew (except for the film's stars—they never set foot on the river) before filming was completed in late 1927. Unfortunately, the film was caught up in disputes between the various owners of the film company, was never completed, and finally was left to languish in a forgotten film archive.

The *Denver Post* was the next to try and market pictures made on a river trip. In 1928 they sponsored an expedition down the "previously unexplored" canyon of the Yampa River, the main tributary of the Green. One of the boats was lost, one man was injured, food, cameras, and much exposed film was washed away—and circulation increased. The pictures that did survive, however, were some of the first to be published of the remote, beautiful canyons of the Yampa.

By the 1930s, cameras were standard equipment on most river trips. Norm Nevills went to great lengths, including finding film (hard to obtain during World War II) to accommodate photographers, as well as movie cameramen, on all of his river trips starting in 1938. Nevills was as interested in the publicity afforded by the films and photos as he was in contributing to history, but the many hundreds of photos made of his trips provide an invaluable record of many places that were forever changed by the dams built in the 1950s. Otis Marston, who accompanied Nevills on many trips during the 1940s, made a number of documentary films which he later narrated and took on the lecture circuit. *Danger River*, a film about Nevills made during a trip on the San Juan River, won an Academy Award for the best short documentary in 1947.

In 1938, free-lance photographer Amos Burg persuaded Buzz Holmstrom to duplicate a solo run he had taken down the Green and the Colorado the year before. Burg would accompany him and film the trip; then they would sell the film and story rights and split the profits. Although they had a fine river trip, and Burg did put together many fabulous films and photographs, little financial gain was ever realized by either one of them.

The years after World War II saw such an explosion in river running, both commercial and private, that, with a few exceptions, photographs of the Colorado and the Green were no longer unique. Some film-makers, ranging from major studios such as Fox-Movietone to independents like Al Morton, continued to make newsreels, travelogues, and even an occasional feature film, but national interests had turned elsewhere. When plans for the Colorado River Storage Project were finalized in the late 1950s, it caused a new rush to see and photograph the canyons that would be flooded by the dams. The pictures taken then, and earlier photographs and films, are all that are left to remind us of the canyons that one photographer called "the place no one knew."

John K. Hillers at Work on the Aquarius Plateau, 1873

Hillers was a native of Germany and a veteran of the American Civil War. In 1871, while working as a teamster in Salt Lake City, he was hired by John Wesley Powell to be a boatman and handyman on Powell's second expedition down the Colorado River. Hillers replaced Jack Sumner, the only member of the first crew to be asked to serve on the second, when Sumner was delayed by spring snows and couldn't make the rendezvous. Hillers served as a boatman and camp helper for most of the trip and often enlivened the camp with his sense of humor and his fine tenor voice. The expedition left the river in the autumn of 1871 to establish winter quarters in Kanab, Utah, planning to resume the river survey the following summer. The photographer, E. O. Beaman of New York City, had had too many differences of opinion with Major Powell, however, and resigned. A replacement photographer, James Fennemore of Salt Lake City, lasted only a few months before ill health forced his departure. The photographers assistant, Walter C. Powell, the Major's young cousin, tried to fill in but could never master the clumsy wet-plate process in use at the time. Clem Powell (as he was called) hated carrying the camera around, calling it the "infernal mountain howitzer." The job finally fell to Hillers, who, as it turned out, was a natural photographer. He made over 3,000 images for the Powell survey and later became official photographer for the U.S.G.S. and the Smithsonian Institution.

Timothy O'Sullivan's Boat, the *Picture*, on the Lower Colorado, 1871

Timothy O'Sullivan got his start as a photographer during the Civil War under Matthew Brady; in fact, some scholars believe that many of the images of that war credited to Brady were actually taken by O'Sullivan and other photographers. O'Sullivan first came west with Clarence King's Geological Survey of the 40th Parallel and stayed with King from 1868 to 1869. While with the King survey, O'Sullivan took some of the first photographs of the rugged country around Browns Park and the remote Yampa River canyons. In 1870 O'Sullivan was the photographer for a survey of the rugged Darien peninsula of Panama.

The next year, O'Sullivan signed on as the photographer for Lt. George M. Wheeler's Geographical Survey West of the 100th Meridian. In 1871, Wheeler decided to ascend the Col-

orado, starting from near Needles, California, and planning to get as far up into the Grand Canyon as he could. The party consisted of seven scientists, six soldiers from Camp Mohave, and fourteen Mohave Indians. For five weeks they toiled in the relentless desert heat, dragging three loaded rowboats, including O'Sullivan's *Picture*, shown here, upstream through Black Canyon, Boulder Canyon, and into the lower Grand Canyon. They hauled their heavy boats and equipment *upstream* past those dreaded falls, Lava Cliff and Separation Rapids, and finally reached the mouth of Diamond Creek around the middle of October. Deciding that they had gone far enough to upstage John Wesley Powell (Wheeler's rival), Wheeler split the party for the return trip. The scientists walked out on the Diamond Creek trail, while the rest of the men ran the boats back downstream to Camp Mohave in a tenth of the time it had taken them to come up. O'Sullivan is a shadowy figure; no known photograph of him exists.

Franklin A. Nims, Photographer for the Brown-Stanton Survey, at Lees Ferry, Christmas 1889

Nims, a photographer from Colorado Springs, Colorado, was hired to document the rail-road survey of the Denver, Colorado Canyon, and Pacific Railway Co. down the Green and Colorado rivers. Nims took many fine photographs before Brown and two others drowned in Marble Canyon and the survey was abandoned in July 1889. When Stanton came back in December of that year to finish the job, Nims, despite the disasters that had plagued the company, agreed to resume his place as the official photographer. On New Years Day, 1890, Nims climbed to a ledge above the river to get a good shot, made the classic photographer's mistake—stepping backwards off the ledge—and fell about twenty feet. One leg and numerous smaller bones were broken, and his skull was fractured. Stanton, ever the engineer, worried first about finishing the survey without a photographer and next about evacuating the badly injured Nims from the canyon. Mercifully, Nims was unconscious and remained so while the crew pushed and pulled him on a stretcher made of oars and blankets 1,800 feet up a side canyon to the rim. He finally regained consciousness at Lonely Dell, the residence of the ferryman for Lees Ferry. A few days later, a passing Mormon family agreed to take him to Winslow, Arizona, where there was a railroad. After another nine days of being jolted in the back of a wagon, Nims reached Winslow, where a doctor was forced to rebreak some of the fractures so they could be properly set. It was almost six months before Nims could walk unaided. To add insult to his injuries, the Denver, Colorado Canyon, and Pacific cut off his salary as of January 1, 1890—the day he fell from the cliff.

Charles Silver Russell on His Boat *Utah,* February 1908

Charles Silver Russell was a wandering prospector, itinerant mining promoter, and part-time newspaper publisher. In 1907, he decided to float the Colorado River through the Grand Canyon, ostensibly on a prospecting trip. In reality, it was a publicity stunt—Russell planned to sell the story and pictures to newspapers across the country. After hiring Bert Loper as photographer, Russell and his partner, Edwin Monett, set out from Green River, Utah, in September 1907. The trip was plagued by difficulty from the start; the trip through Cataract Canyon was very difficult, with capsizes and near-misses the whole way. In the process, Loper's camera got wet and the shutter rusted shut. Russell and Monett agreed to wait at Lees Ferry while Loper went for a replacement. When he took too long getting back, however, Russell left without him. This was a big mistake, as Loper was the only one with any boating experience. Monett, who was worse than a novice in a boat, capsized twice in Cataract Canyon, once in Marble Canyon, and finally hung his boat on a rock in Grand Canyon and lost it altogether. Loper, when he finally made it to Lees Ferry and found his companions had left without him, rowed and pulled his boat 170 miles back up through Glen Canyon to Hite. Russell and Monett, meanwhile, finally made it through the Grand Canyon, although Russell reportedly had to threaten Monett with a revolver to get him back in the remaining boat. They reached Needles, California, in February 1908, with no film, no prospects, and one leaky boat of the three they had started out with. Monett promptly disappeared, and Russell went back to prospecting, but the Colorado was still on his mind.

Ellsworth and Emery Kolb on the *Defiance*, 1911

The Kolb brothers had a photography studio on the South Rim of the Grand Canyon and made their living selling photographs to tourists. They had a greater goal, however: to make a complete photographic record of the canyons of the Green and the Colorado. While they were good photographers, the brothers were enthusiastic but completely inexperienced river runners. Undeterred, they had two boats built to specifications given them by Julius Stone and set off down the Green River in September 1911. Ellsworth was the elder, and the more daredevil of the two. Characteristically, he named his boat *Defiance*, while Emery named his *Edith* for his young daughter. The brothers floated down the rivers, taking photos and films as they went and learning how to handle a boat in rough water. They made it all the way into the Grand Canyon with no problems other than an occasional bump or scrape, although Ellsworth flipped both boats trying to become the first to run Soap Creek rapid. In Walthenberg Rapid, just below the Bass trail, both brothers upset at the same time. The *Edith* suffered some damage, but it was soon repaired, and they reached Needles, California, in January 1912. To complete the trip, Ellsworth returned to Needles in May 1913 and in an old skiff rode the spring rise of the Colorado all the way to the gulf of California. In this photograph, Ellsworth is on the stern deck demonstrating the way passengers were forced to ride through rapids in the days before big inflatable boats. Small wonder that most early passengers on river trips chose to walk around rapids.

August Tadje, Erstwhile Cameraman for Charles Russell, on the Deck of the *Titanic II*, 1914

After hearing of the success of the Kolb brothers' film and book about their 1911 river run, Charles Russell decided to try once again to make a film about the Colorado. Again he hired Bert Loper as boatman, and they started from Green River in two steel-framed boats in July 1914. In Cataract Canyon, while Loper waited on shore with a movie camera, hoping for a dramatic scene to film, Russell ran Rapid #14. He got more than he bargained for, as it turned out—Russell flipped the boat, which promptly sank beneath the brown water. Shaken, they stashed the remaining boat and made their way over the desert to Green River. Russell left to secure a cameraman, more funding, cameras, and supplies; in the meantime, Loper took a job with the U.S.G.S. at the confluence of the Green and the Colorado. When Russell got back to Green River and found Loper gone, he took Loper's boat, saying that

Bert owed him money anyway, and headed downriver. When Russell and the new camera-man, August Tadje of Salt Lake City, got to the confluence, Loper and Russell promptly got into a fistfight over who owed what to whom. Russell and Tadje continued on, struggling through Cataract Canyon, chopping their boat out of the ice in Glen Canyon. They lost three more boats and changed helpers three times before they finally reached the Grand Canyon. And it was all for naught—as they tried to retrieve one of the boats which Russell had stuck in the rocks at Crystal Rapid, it overturned and spilled its contents—cameras, exposed film, food and camp gear, foolishly left in the boat—into the river. It was too much even for Russell, and the project was abandoned once and for all. Russell never ran the river again.

Ellsworth Kolb, 1914

In addition to the 8 × 10 glass plate camera pictured here, in 1911 the Kolb brothers took a 5 × 7 plate camera, three film cameras, a portable darkroom, and most important, a hand-cranked movie camera. The Kolbs were no strangers to the hardships of scenic photography, having hiked all over the Grand Canyon to take pictures. And they were in good physical condition; at their South Rim studio, there was no water source, so to develop pictures taken of tourists leaving on the morning mule train, they had to run down a different trail to Indian Gardens, halfway down into the Grand Canyon, develop the film, and run back up the trail before the mule train got back in the evening. The movie camera was an entirely new development in river running, and although the mechanism was delicate and they often had to disassemble the camera to dry parts that got wet in rapids, the film they made was the first ever shot of river running. Sometimes it could get them into trouble. Ellsworth wanted to get a movie of the first run of Soap Creek rapid, so he put Emery on shore with the movie camera and pushed off into the current. In the monster waves at top of the rapid, Ellsworth promptly capsized. Ignoring his brother's advice that they line the other boat, Ellsworth tried again. This time he was thrown from the boat, caught his foot on the gunwale, and almost drowned before Emery could rescue him. Despite these misadventures, the trip was a success; their South Rim studio was filled with shots taken on that and later trips. Both brothers became recognized authorities on river running, and went on many more trips over the years. Ellsworth moved back to Pennsylvania in the 1920s for a time,

but he spent much of his later life in Los Angeles, where he died in 1960. Emery stayed at the Grand Canyon the rest of his life. The motion picture they made was shown almost daily in their studio until Emery died in 1976, making it one of the longest running commercial films ever produced. Literally thousands of people from all over the world were introduced to the Colorado River by the film, their photographs, and Ellsworth's delightful book about their adventures, *Through the Grand Canyon from Wyoming to Mexico*.

E. C. LaRue and Panorama Camera at Vasey's Paradise, Marble Canyon, 1923

E. C. LaRue, hydrologist and co-leader of the U.S.G.S. Grand Canyon survey, was also the official cameraman. When the crew met at Lees Ferry at the start of the expedition, however, LaRue discovered that Emery Kolb, hired as head boatman, also planned to take pictures during the trip. LaRue stiffly informed Kolb that he (LaRue) was the official photographer, and only he would be allowed to take photographs, which would be the exclusive property of the U.S. government anyway. Sparks flew; Kolb told LaRue what he could do with his camera, that he could row his own boats down the Grand Canyon, and resigned on the spot. Cooler heads prevailed, however, and a compromise was reached. Kolb was allowed to bring one small camera and take pictures, provided that the U.S.G.S. got first rights to them. Friction between Kolb and LaRue didn't end there, however, and there was another blowup at the Hermit Trail, less than a third of the way down the canyon. Again, Kolb told LaRue he was resigning. Fine, LaRue told him, pick up your wages; Frank Dodge could row his boat. Kolb's family was there, having come down the Hermit Trail to watch the party run Hermit Rapid. Edith, Kolb's daughter, fainted from the excitement and had to be carried back up the trail to their camp. This time the other boatmen, realizing that the most difficult rapids were still to come, and Mrs. Kolb, not wanting to lose the wages, prevailed on LaRue and Kolb to shake hands and make up. This they did, and Emery finished the trip, but there was no love lost between LaRue and Kolb for the rest of the trip.

Chester and Kenneth Wortley of the Lasky Party, in Glen Canyon, 1924

Chester Wortley was a cameraman for movie mogul Cecil B. DeMille; his brother Ken was an outdoor packer and guide. Together with Jesse L. Lasky, vice president for production of Paramount Pictures, they took a number of trips on the Colorado River. They floated Glen Canyon from Hite to Lees Ferry and from Needles to Yuma, California. On another occasion they went from Yuma all the way downriver, through the wild delta of the Colorado to the Gulf of California. Lasky and the Wortley brothers also made a first descent of the Balsas River in Mexico. Sometimes it was just the three friends; on other trips they were accompanied by DeMille himself and Zane Grey, the western writer. On these and other trips, Chester Wortley, a professional cameraman, made movies of their experiences, using the high-quality movie camera shown here. The films were made just for the enjoyment of the participants, though, and are now either languishing in a forgotten film vault somewhere or are lost altogether.

Weatherhead & Dow · Eddy · Holt · Galloway
Seager · Adger · Eartl · Race · Carey · Callaway

Clyde Eddy Party, Grand Canyon, 1927

Clyde Eddy, a veteran of the trenches in World War I, took a trip down the Hermit Trail to the bottom of the Grand Canyon with his wife shortly after the war. Taking one look at the Colorado, he decided that it was "his" river, and that he would someday run it and make a documentary film about the journey. Casting about for sponsors, Eddy managed to interest the International Newsreel Co. and Metro-Goldwyn-Mayer enough that the former agreed to provide a cameraman and film. For a guide and boatman, Eddy hired Parley Galloway (son of Nathaniel), who had learned to run rivers at his father's knee. The crew was chosen by mail from among scores of applicants, "pink-wristed" college men who answered Eddy's ad in newspapers around the country. To give the film some human interest, Eddy added a black bear cub bought from a traveling circus and a stray dog from the Salt Lake City pound. The bear was named Cataract and the dog, "mostly airedale," was christened Rags. Eddy had three sturdy boats built on the Powell model, round-bottomed and with deep drafts. They started from Green River, Utah, on the spring flood. Probably a mistake: the high water in Cataract Canyon completely unnerved three of the crew, among them the newsreel cameraman, who hadn't wanted to go in the first place. All three left at Lees Ferry. Eddy managed to secure a replacement of sorts, in the person of an itinerant drifter who happened to have a hand-held 8mm movie camera. They proceeded cautiously into the Grand Canyon, and even made the first run of Soap Creek Rapid, albeit inadvertently—Eddy didn't realize they had run Soap Creek until later. At Dubendorff Rapid, however, while they were trying to line one of the heavy boats past the fall, it got away and was pinned hopelessly against a rock. Jamming the crew and the remaining supplies into the other two boats, they made the rest of the trip in the searing, numbing heat of August. No commercial movie resulted from the trip, even though the films still exist. Eddy did publish an account, dramatically titled *Down the World's Most Dangerous River*. It was the beginning of a lifelong obsession with the Colorado for Clyde Eddy.

Cast and Crew of *Bride of the Colorado*, 1927

The Pathe-Bray movie company was formed to produce a film about the Colorado River, hoping to take advantage of the publicity generated by the Bureau of Reclamation's recently announced decision to build a dam below the Grand Canyon. In charge of the crew assigned to float the river and make the film was none other than E. C. LaRue, who had recently lost his job with the U.S.G.S. as a result of a bitter dispute over where to build the dam (LaRue wanted it in Glen Canyon, just above Lees Ferry). The film crew ran Cataract Canyon first, taking background shots, and caused a brief flurry of excitement in the canyon country when they fell behind schedule in Glen Canyon and were presumed lost. They

then moved into the Grand Canyon, where the boatmen (including Frank Dodge) acted as doubles for the stars, who never actually ran a rapid. The climatic rescue scene was shot at Hermit Rapid. The boatmen/stuntmen ran the rapid again and again, dragging the heavy boats back upstream each time for yet another take. Chilled by the icy water—it was now December—the boatmen almost perished from exposure and spent their time between takes trying to warm themselves around driftwood fires and cursing all cameramen everywhere. All their hard work was to no avail, however; the partners in the movie company fell into a dispute over who owned the rights, and the film was never released.

Denver Post "Exploration" of the Yampa River, 1928

In the newspaper business the "dog days" of August are traditionally a slow news period; editors will do almost anything, including making news stories out of whole cloth, to increase circulation. In the summer of 1928, the editor of the *Denver Post* did just that. He sent a crew consisting of A. G. Birch, Fred Dunham, Charles Mace, and Bert Moritz, Jr., to "explore" the "unknown canyons" of the Yampa River, the major tributary of the Green. None the men had any experience with rivers, and the two boats, the *Leakin' Lena* and the *Prickly Heat*, were clumsy and ill-suited for the Yampa at the low water of late summer. As Dock Marston later wrote, they were "obviously due for adventure." The trip was an unqualified disaster—to the editor's delight—and *Post* readers were thrilled for two weeks with lurid headlines detailing the mishaps befalling the crew. One boat was lost early on, with much of their food and cooking gear. Birch was injured trying to free one of the boats, and later the cameras and much exposed film was dumped overboard, which almost "made the men weep." After the shore party following along the rim of the canyon lost sight of them, a rescue party was mounted. In the meantime, however, the river crew abandoned the remaining boat at the Mantle Ranch at Castle Park and walked out.

Lining Soap Creek Rapid, 1934

During the era of wooden riverboats, such as this Galloway-style skiff being lined around Soap Creek, rapids were not run with the aplomb that they are in today's inflatable craft. Wooden boats are much more delicate, comparatively speaking, and while they make fine river craft in the hands of a skilled oarsman, they are not forgiving of mistakes. A mishap in a wooden boat could mean damage that might take days to repair. Worse yet, a serious mis-calculation could mean a wrecked or lost boat and a long walk back to civilization. To avoid such possibilities, especially when low water exposed the rocks in the channel, most early parties lined the bigger rapids. This involved unloading the boat and letting it down alongside the rapid with ropes attached to bow and stern. Usually one man stayed in the boat to push it off rocks. The supplies and equipment were then carried past the rapid and reloaded. On some stretches this had to be repeated every mile or so, much to the dismay of the crews. Lining was an arduous, time-consuming, and sometimes dangerous procedure—at best, the men would suffer barked shins and twisted ankle; at worst, they would be dragged into the river. Sometimes the boat would get away from the men on shore and be swept into the rapids or lost altogether. As an alternative—besides just running the rapid, unthinkable at the time—boats were occasionally turned loosed and allowed to run a rapid empty, often with disastrous results. Small wonder, then, that this was one of the last times that the Hatch-Swain party lined their boats in the Grand in 1934. The process is being filmed in this photo by Fred Jayne, a cameraman brought along by Clyde Eddy for the 1934 journey.

The *Deseret News* Crew on the Yampa, 1937

Although Major Powell had rowed twelve miles up the Yampa from its mouth in 1871, and Nathaniel Galloway ran it with his 9-year-old son Parley in 1909, this main tributary of the Green was still largely unknown in 1928 when the *Denver Post* sponsored its highly publicized expedition to "explore" the Yampa.

Nine years later Charles Kelly, a veteran of several previous river trips, decided to go down the Yampa and see what the fuss was about. He called up some friends, including Henry Millecam, a dentist from Salt Lake City, Hack Miller, a columnist from the *Deseret News*, Dr. Russ Frazier of Bingham, Utah, and seasoned rivermen Alt Hatch and Royce "Cap" Mowrey of Vernal. They made the eighty-mile trip down the Yampa from Lily Park, Colorado, to Jensen, Utah, in fine style. Kelly noted that the trip was little more than a pleasure cruise with good boats and good boatmen and said that he would "go again tomorrow."

The Burg-Holmstrom Party at Camp, 1938

After Buzz Holmstrom's solo traverse of the Green and Colorado rivers in 1937, an article about him appeared in the *Saturday Evening Post*. The article caught the eye of Amos Burg, a free-lance photographer and film maker. Burg was also an experienced river runner; he had been on the Mississippi and rivers in Oregon and Idaho. Burg contacted Holmstrom and proposed that they go down the river together, duplicating Buzz's earlier feat. Burg would make a film of the journey, they would sell the story and film rights and split the profits. Buzz was agreeable—anything was better than working in a gas station—so they started out from the source of the Green, the Green River lakes in Wyoming. Not enough water, though, so a passing cowboy agreed to haul their boats to the town of Green River, Wyoming, and they started over. With them in this photograph is Willis Johnson (center), who joined them at Green River, Utah. Buzz was in his handmade wooden boat, now graced with a new coat of red paint and named *Julius F.* after Julius Stone, whose last-minute check to Holmstrom made the trip possible. Burg, however, was rowing something never before seen on the river—an inflatable boat named the *Charlie* that Burg had built to his specifications by the Goodyear Rubber Co. Buzz Holmstrom, meanwhile, was after a first of his own. This time he ran every rapid on the river and became the first person ever to do so. Burg had to line the *Charlie* a few times, since it had an embarrassing tendency to fold up in a

rapid. They reached Boulder Dam in November 1938. Burg did put together a film of their voyage, and while it was never a commercial success, it is a remarkable record of Holmstrom's skill with the oars. Few boatmen will ever be his equal.

Genevieve DeColmont Filming her Husband in His Kayak, 1938

Genevieve, her husband Bernard, and a companion, Antoine DeSeyne, came to the United States in the summer of 1938 to run the Green and the Colorado in their fifteen-foot folding kayaks. Bernard was a photographer for the Paris Museum of Natural History, and his ambition was to make a film of a journey down the Green and the Colorado through the Grand Canyon. He brought a battery of cameras, both still and motion-picture. Antoine DeSeyne also brought a small movie camera, and together they took hundreds of feet of footage in both black and white and color, as well as many still photos. The usual procedure in especially difficult rapids was for Bernard, the only experienced kayaker, to run all three craft through while Genevieve and Antoine took movies and still photos. The DeColmonts published a small book of their photographs, titled *Trois Francais in Kayak sur le Colorado*, upon their return home to France in early 1939. The color film produced and narrated by Bernard was shown many times in France and was very well received, but in the turmoil of the war and the German occupation, was never seen in this country until the 1980s. In this photo, Genevieve is filming her husband as he runs one of the rapids in the Canyon of Lodore on the Green River.

The Fox-Movietone Rainbow Bridge Expedition in Glen Canyon, 1945

In September 1944 the Fox-Movietone newsreel company hired Norm Nevills, by then a well-known river outfitter, to take a film crew down the San Juan River to Glen Canyon. Fox planned to make a short subject about the journey, including footage of Rainbow Bridge. Although World War II was still raging, Americans were weary of war news and Fox was trying for something different to divert movie audiences. Nevills was the obvious choice to pilot them down the river; he had been running the San Juan since 1934, and had taken hundreds of men, women, and children down it safely. Nevills was always eager for good publicity for his growing river business and was happy to oblige. September often produces storms in the San Juan country, however, and occasional floods. The water was high when they set off, and to Nevills' mortification, on the first day one of his boatmen capsized and lost an expensive film camera such as the one shown. The cameraman and producer, who also lost their clothing and other equipment, called it quits and hiked out of the canyon. They tried again the next year, however, and this time made it all the way down the San Juan with boats and cameras intact. Fox-Movietone made a twenty-minute color travel film about the trip, which was later released as *Along the Rainbow Trail*.

Al Morton on the *Moviemaker*

Alton Morton was a native of Midway, Utah. He began taking amateur movies while he worked as a letter carrier for the U.S. Post Office, but was soon making commissioned travelogues for the Utah State Tourist and Publicity Council. In the late 1940s he got acquainted with Don Harris and Jack Brennan, then on the river with an outfit called Harris-Brennan River Expeditions. Morton made several movies with them; the films are well made and enjoyable, and were shown as part of the effort to increase tourism in the state after World War II. Harris and Brennan usually ran powerboat trips, Harris with his faithful *Mexican Hat*, which he had built with Norm Nevills in 1938, and Brennan in a boat of similar design named *Adventurer*. Later, as he made more and more trips with them, Morton decided he needed his own boat, so with the help of his two river companions, he built the *Moviemaker*. Like Harris' and Brennan's boats, it was a modified cataract design. Morton, like many river runners of the time, could not abide the idea of inflatable rafts—derisively called "baloney boats"—on the same river he was on, and refused to have anything to do with them. Al Morton and his films were often a feature at meetings of the Western River Guides Association, a Salt Lake-based river runners group.

Les Jones at the Oars of His Modified Canoe, *Honey—The Rapids Queen*

Leslie Jones, a civil engineer from Heber City, Utah, started running rivers in 1953 when he helped his cousin Don Hatch (son of riverman Bus Hatch) organize float trips for the Sierra Club. Not content with the inflatable craft that were just coming into common use and uncomfortable with crowds (seventy-five passengers were not uncommon on Sierra Club trips), Jones designed and built his own boat and ran rivers in small groups or solo. *Honey*, like most of Jones' boats, was a decked-over, oar-rigged canoe, reinforced with watertight bulkheads. Since he ran solo, he devised a way to take pictures, shown in this photo. Jones mounted a camera on a football helmet, then covered it with an inverted paint can for

protection—the spotlight was for shady areas. The shutter was tripped by a remote release bulb that he held in his mouth. To take a shot, he pointed his head and bit on the bulb. In 1954 and 1955, Jones ran Cataract Canyon by himself, before Lake Powell had covered up the worst rapids. In 1957, he soloed the Grand Canyon. That same year, he rowed—again by himself—from the Gates of Lodore to the mouth of Split Mountain Canyon, almost fifty miles of rocks and rapids, in less than ten hours, stopping to chat with the ranger at Echo Park on the way. When the gates of Glen Canyon Dam were closed in 1963, and the Colorado was reduced to a trickle, Jones and Ulrich Martin, a champion German kayaker, ran the Grand Canyon at record low water. For that run, Jones used another of his custom boats, a 19-inch-wide aluminum kayak. Jones later became well known for the beautiful scroll maps he made of many western rivers.

Charles Eggert and Fellow Travelers, Lake Mead, 1956

Fred Wood, Charles Eggert, and Bruce Lium were the only three members of the 1955 John Wesley Powell commemorative trip to run the entire length of the Green and Colorado Rivers; and they were the last to do so, for by the time they finished their voyage at Temple Bar on Lake Mead in June 1956, construction had begun on Glen Canyon Dam. Eggert, a film-maker from New York, was involved with the Sierra Club and National Park Service in their fight against the Echo Park Dam in the late 1940s and early 1950s. In 1952, while producing a film titled "This Is Dinosaur" for the Park Service, Eggert met Don Hatch, son of famed riverman Bus Hatch. Don and Bus guided Eggert around the remote canyons of the Green and Yampa so that he could obtain film footage. While sitting with Don overlooking the entrance of Lodore Canyon, Eggert remarked how he would love to follow Powell's journey all the way from Wyoming through the Grand Canyon. Don replied "Well, Charlie, maybe one day we'll find a reason to do it."

Three years later they had found their reason, and the party set off from Green River, Wyoming, on June 11, 1955. Other members of the party were Fred Wood, co-leader; Don Hatch, co-leader and head boatman; Bruce Lium, boatman; Leslie Jones, boatman; Tony Tuttle, Eggert's assistant photographer; Mrs. Cyd Ricketts Sumner, an author; and Dr. Robert Parsons. The personnel changed constantly; Don Hatch, for instance, left the trip

reluctantly from Phantom Ranch to lead a first descent of the Indus River in Pakistan for Lowell Thomas. Cyd Rickets Sumner later wrote a book called *Traveler in the Wilderness*, about her experiences as "one woman among seven rugged men." Eggert's two films about the expedition—*A Canyon Voyage* and *"Danger River"*—are a fitting tribute to Glen Canyon and the other marvelous wonders which were forever lost under the waters of the big reservoirs.

CHAPTER 4
Adventurers

I have already had my reward, in the doing of the things, the starts, cliffs, and canyons, the roar of the rapids, the moon, the uncertainty and worry, the relieve when thro each one—the campfires at night— the real respect and friendship of the rivermen I met.

—Buzz Holmstrom, 1937

Until the beginning of the twentieth century, the idea of running the Colorado solely for adventure rarely entered anyone's mind, and if it did, they would hardly admit it. River running was something strong men did only after they had written out their wills. Although an element of danger and adventure entered into any trip down the river, men ran the Colorado and the Green for furs, for gold, for science—not for thrills.

By 1909, however, that attitude had begun to change. That summer two young college athletes from St. Louis, Missouri, named Tom Martin and Jules Woodward set out from Green River, Wyoming, to run the rapids of the Green in a special steel boat. About a week later, they stumbled back into town, naked and sunburned and scratched. The river took their boat, their food, and even their clothes in Red Canyon, and they had been forced to walk sixty miles across the desert to reach town.

A few months later, Julius Stone began what was the first well-planned and well-executed trip undertaken solely for pleasure. Stone wanted to run the river ostensibly to check up on John Wesley Powell's account of his pioneering voyage and take photographs of the canyons. Really, though, Stone ran the river just because he was intrigued by it; he was a tourist. His cruise was the first of what would become thousands of recreational trips down the Green and Colorado.

The Kolb brothers, Ellsworth and Emery, were next. Again, their avowed purpose was to take photos and films, and indeed they did. Unlike Stone, however, they went without a guide—Stone had hired Nathaniel Galloway as his guide and boatman—even though neither of them had ever rowed a boat through rapids before. This lack of experience made adventure and mishaps not only likely but inevitable.

Inspired by the Kolb's book about their experiences, *Through the Grand Canyon from Wyoming to Mexico*, which was published in 1914, others began to try their hands at river running. That same year a young man from Jensen, Utah, named Jens Jensen, ran the upper Green from Lodore to Split Mountain "just for fun." In the years before World War I and into the 1920s, a number of adventurers floated Glen Canyon in folding canvas canoes owned out by long-time guide Dave Rust. Rust would usually accompany the people as their guide, but often people preferred to go on their own. In 1926, three college chums from Princeton, out on a lark, took boats from Green River, Wyoming, to Green River, Utah.

The 1930s saw an explosion in river running for the sake of adventure. Beginning in 1932, Charles Kelly, the western historian and writer, took numerous trips on the Colorado, the Green, the Yampa, and Idaho's Salmon River. Another who got started around the same time was Dr. Russell Frazier, the company doctor for Utah Copper Co. in Bingham, Utah. Dr. Frazier wasn't much good at handling a boat, but he was willing and adventurous and, more important, had money to finance trips. Buzz Holmstrom made the first, and one of the only, solo runs of the river in 1937, a feat done for adventure above all else.

During the decade, the first kayaks—wooden-framed foldboats with a waterproof canvas hull—were used on both the Green and the Colorado. There were the French kayakers, Bernard and Genevieve DeColmont and Antoine DeSeyne; Genevieve was the first woman to pilot her own boat down the Green and the Colorado. Stewart Gardiner and Alexander "Zee" Grant rounded out what had been a busy decade for river running by taking foldboats through the upper canyons of the Green in 1938 and 1939. Grant took his kayak through the Grand Canyon with Norm Nevills in 1941. After the war, kayaking also became more popular, with such greats as Roger Paris and Walter Kirschbaum on the river. Women began to kayak as well; in 1953 a woman named Nora Staley kayaked the Canyon of Lodore, with Don Hatch along in an inflatable raft for support.

During the first few years of the 1940s, river running dropped off sharply as America's energies were tied up in the cataclysm of World War II. After the war, however, the number of recreational river runners quickly reached and surpassed the levels of the 1930s. There were a number of factors involved in the increase—cars, tires, and gasoline, rationed during the war, were now available—but the most important was also the most basic: boats. It took a lot of skill and experience to successfully pilot a wooden riverboat through heavy rapids. Wooden boats were not forgiving of error, so the only people who became proficient at river running were those who for the most part did little else—commercial river guides. When the war ended, high-quality surplus inflatable rafts became widely available at a price anyone could afford, and suddenly virtually anyone could run rapids. If the raft hit a rock, generally it just bounced off. If you capsized in a rapid, you just righted the raft and continued on. There were, and still are, those who prefer wooden boats through a sense of adventure, or closeness with the river, or pride in a vanishing heritage. But by the 1960s most people who ran the Colorado or the Green did it in an inflatable raft.

In the 1950s river running as a sport continued its upward surge. Thousands of tourists from the Sierra Club, the Boy Scouts, and other groups, as well as individuals, flocked to see the canyons that were threatened by the Colorado River Storage Project. By the early 1960s recreational (i.e., noncommercial, or as they are commonly known, "privates") boaters were an established part of the river-running world. When the National Park Service and other government agencies charged with managing recreational use of the Colorado and the Green established a permit system to regulate use in the 1970s, private river runners were part of the mix and were given a percentage of the permits. Today the upward trend has slowed somewhat, but the signs indicate that those who want to run the river on their own, like the Kolb brothers, will be on the Colorado for a long time to come.

The *Major Powell* After Being Abandoned, 1894

The smooth waters of the Green River near the town of the same name in Utah have long offered an inducement to boaters. Green River was settled in 1883; within less than a decade the first powered boats were chugging up and down the river. The first, a thirty-five-foot steam- powered launch named the *Major Powell*, was launched in 1891. B. S. Ross formed the Green, Grand, and Colorado River Excursion Company to run tourists down the river to a hotel to be built at the confluence with the Grand, as the Colorado was known before 1922. The maiden voyage ended at the mouth of the San Rafael river, only twenty-three miles below town, when the boat lost her propellers on a submerged rock. The next year another attempt was made; this time they made it to the confluence, but on the return journey ran out of coal, and the boat was tied up on the riverbank. Ross, discouraged, dropped out of the scheme. William Edwards bought the abandoned boat, made some repairs, and tried again in March 1893. This time they made it all the way to the confluence and back, in only two weeks. Edwards was enthusiastic about the prospects but admitted that the *Major Powell* was too small and underpowered for what he had in mind. Finding no backers willing to finance a bigger craft, however, Edwards abandoned the idea—and the *Major Powell*. In 1894, she was bought by four men who stripped out her engines and boiler to use in a mining operation and scrapped her hull. The little launch had only been down the river three times, but she had proved it could be done.

Julius Stone at Separation Canyon, 1939

Julius Stone, the wealthy industrialist who helped finance the Hoskaninni Mining Co., met Nathaniel Galloway while inspecting his investment in Glen Canyon. Galloway was working for the company as a boatman and hunter, and guided Stone up and down the canyon. Later, Galloway took Stone hunting in the Henry Mountains, and the two—millionaire from Ohio and trapper from Utah—became good friends. When Stone began to plan his grand traverse of the Green and Colorado rivers in 1909, he asked Galloway to be the guide. Moreover, he brought Galloway back to Ohio to design and oversee the construction of the four boats. Stone himself made some suggestions; the resulting craft are known as Galloway-Stone boats. Other members of the party were C. C. Sharp, an attorney and friend of Stone's; Raymond Cogswell, Stone's brother-in-law and the photographer; Galloway; and Seymour

Dubendorff, a friend of Galloway's. They left Green River, Wyoming in September 1909; on board, besides the supplies they had brought, was a quart of rye whiskey given them by a local man in case they had an accident and needed a general anesthetic. Despite the low water of the early autumn they made good time, with very few mishaps. It was an enchanting trip, according to Stone; although he said he was going on the trip to make a photographic record of the canyons, he was really doing it for the same reasons that thousands of recreational river runners did who followed him. The party reached Needles, California, in November, with the bottle of whiskey, unopened. Julius Stone retained an interest in the Colorado River for the rest of his life.

Seymour Dubendorff at Split Mountain, 1909

When Julius Stone was looking for boatmen for his trip down the Green and Colorado rivers in 1909, his guide Nathaniel Galloway recommended Seymour Dubendorff. Dubendorff lived in Myton, Utah, where he worked in the gilsonite mines. Unlike his friend Galloway,

however, "Dubie," as he was called, had no experience on rivers. He was, as Stone noted, dependable, cheerful, strong, and "gritty as a flapjack rolled in sand." At first Galloway ran all the boats through the rapids, but as they went on, the others gained experience and ran more and more on their own. Dubendorff capsized a boat in Cataract Canyon, but he learned fast and had no more trouble until he tried to run an unnamed fall at mile 132 in the Grand Canyon. At the top of the rapid, his boat overturned and threw him into the river. Galloway caught the boat while Dubendorff swam to shore. Blood was streaming from a cut on his scalp where he had hit his head as the boat capsized, but Dubendorff was more embarrassed than hurt. Let me try it again; I know I can do it right this time, he begged Galloway. Nathaniel decided, however, that enough was enough, and he ran the rest of the boats through while Dubendorff was patched up. After that, there were no more mishaps, and all concerned enjoyed the trip so much that they agreed they would go on another the next year. By that time, unfortunately, Dubendorff had died from spotted fever, and the trip never materialized. In 1923, the U.S.G.S. Grand Canyon survey named the rapid that had caused his problem Dubendorff Rapid. The nearby canyon was named for Galloway, and the beautiful creek in its bottom is today known as Stone Creek.

Ellsworth Kolb on the Colorado River, 1916

The Colorado between Grand Junction, Colorado, and Moab, Utah, is easily navigable except for Westwater Canyon, eighteen miles of narrow canyon and dangerous cataracts. When S. S. Harper, an engineer for the Denver, Colorado Canyon, and Pacific Railway floated the river while on a railroad survey in 1889, he hauled his boat around Westwater by wagon. It wasn't until August 1897 that Westwater Canyon was run successfully, by two dentists from Glenwood Springs, Colorado, named Babcock and Miller. They ran the dangerous rapids in a seventeen-foot wooden boat, floated all the way to the head of Cataract Canyon, made their way back upstream, and then, apparently content with river running, never floated again. The next known run of Westwater wasn't until 1916, by that peripatetic river runner, Ellsworth Kolb. After completing the traverse of the Green and the Colorado in May 1913, Ellsworth cast about for new challenges. In August 1916 Kolb and J. W. Shields ran the Colorado from Grand Junction to Cisco, Utah, in a seventeen-foot canoe. Westwater was

too much for them, however, so they portaged their boat around the canyon and then continued on down to Moab. The next year, Ellsworth tried again, this time with Bert Loper as his companion. Ellsworth Kolb and Bert Loper were two of the most experienced rivermen in the West at the time, and experience counts in river running as in everything else. They made the first successful run of Westwater Canyon. Kolb only went as far as Moab before returning to his photo studio, but Loper took the boat all the way down to the confluence with the Green. There he hooked up an outboard motor and made his way back up the river to Moab. Ellsworth and Loper also ran the Dolores River, a tributary of the Colorado, in company with Julius Stone.

The Todd-Page Party on the Upper Green, 1926

When F. Lemoyne Page of New York City decided to try a run of the Green River for an on unusual vacation, the first person he thought of was his school chum from Princeton, Web Todd. As they read accounts of previous expeditions, they discovered that the stretch from Green River, Wyoming, to Green River, Utah, was linked by rail lines that crossed the river at both points. Reading further, they learned that it was also "a real escapade . . . difficult, tedious, and hard." Undeterred, they recruited another college friend, "Og" West, and met in Wyoming in August 1926. There they hired experienced riverman H. E. Blake (late of the U.S.G.S. surveys) as a guide and a local man, Curley Hale, as a camp cook. They bought two boats from the U.S.G.S., made their own life jackets from cork, and set out. It was a grand adventure, and all went well in the upper canyons. One boat lodged on a rock in Red Creek Rapid, but they were able to free it using a makeshift windlass. In Lodore, they made good runs of Disaster Falls, Triplet Falls, and Hell's Half Mile, only to pin one of the boats irretrievably in an unnamed riffle just above Echo Park. Lost with the boat were cameras, film, and personal gear. Echoing the lament of many later river runners, Page wrote, "The high confining walls which had seemed so beautiful and grand a day or so before now almost drove me mad. This disaster had been so unexpected, so unnecessary, so ridiculous." The men were forced to walk around the rest of the rapids all the way to Jensen, Utah. Discouraged, Page left at Jensen, and only Todd, Hale, and Blake continued on through Desolation Canyon to Green River, Utah. The boat was later recovered by Parley Galloway, and proved to be the inspiration for the craft built by that premier riverman, Bus Hatch.

Bessie and Glen Hyde, The "Honeymoon Couple," 1928

Glen Hyde of Twin Falls, Idaho, and Bessie Haley of Washington, D.C., met in Los Angeles in 1927, fell in love, and were married in April 1928. Hearing of the Pathe-Bray movie expedition on the Colorado, Glen came up with a novel idea for a honeymoon. Why not build a boat and float through the Grand Canyon, becoming the first husband and wife team to make the trip? Hyde already had some experience on rivers in British Columbia and Idaho, so, with Bessie's reluctant approval, he decided to give it a try. At Green River, Utah, he built a twenty-foot, flat-bottomed scow, which was steered by two long balance sweeps at bow and stern. It was a type of boat that was in common use on the rivers in Idaho, but had not been seen on the Colorado. Despite dire predictions of disaster—one observer remarked that the boat looked like a coffin—they left from Green River in October, planning to reach Needles, California, in December. Glen managed to get them through Cataract Canyon, only to be warned at Lees Ferry that they were foolish to continue. The weather was cold, the river low; nevertheless, continue they did. They climbed out at the Bright Angel trail and stayed with Emery Kolb and his family for a rest. Departing, Bessie looked longingly at Emery's young daughter and said "I wonder if I'll ever wear pretty shoes again." They were last seen at the foot of the Hermit Trail, when, according to observers, Glen had to force Bessie back into the boat. After they failed to appear at the appointed rendezvous, a massive

search was launched by Glen's father. Their boat was found floating in an eddy in the Lower Granite Gorge, with Bessie's camera and diary aboard. Glen and Bessie were never seen again. Despite the search, no solid clue to the fate of the Honeymoon Couple was ever found, although rumors have come and gone on the river for years. One apocryphal story, widely told around Grand Canyon campfires, concerns an elderly woman, a passenger on a commercial river trip in the canyon almost half a century later. Despite her insistence that she had never been in the canyon, she seemed to have a surprisingly detailed knowledge of canyon and river. Near the end of the trip, according to the story, she revealed to the startled passengers and crew that she was indeed Bessie Hyde. She claimed to have been abused by Glen until finally she killed him in his sleep, hid his body, and climbed out of the canyon. She returned to the east coast, where she lived under an assumed name, never revealing her secret until then.

"Doc" Inglesby in Glen Canyon

Dr. Arthur L. Inglesby was born in Canada in 1872, and trained in dentistry at Northwest University in Chicago. Around 1900, he moved west to practice his profession in the mining towns of Mercur and later Bingham, Utah. Wanting to branch out from dentistry and having a keen interest in geology, he started the Bingham Stage Lines in 1906. Besides basic transportation, Inglesby also offered geologic tours of the West, including Bryce Canyon, Zion Canyon, and other points of interest. For a while he had a partner, Dr. Frederick J. Pack, a professor of geology at the University of Utah. In 1935, Inglesby retired and moved to Fruita, Utah, near Capitol Reef National Park. There he became a full-time rockhound, and also made the acquaintance of a fellow resident of Fruita, Charles Kelly. With Kelly, Doc Inglesby began to take occasional float trips through Glen Canyon and other places. It was on one such trip that this photo was taken. During a later trip on the Green River, Inglesby was accorded an honor that comes to few men in their lifetimes; he had a rapid named after him. While running the last rapid in Split Mountain Canyon, Inglesby was pitched from the boat. The rapid is today known as Inglesby Rapid.

The "Dusty Dozen," 1934

In 1934, Dr. Russell Frazier, a company doctor from Bingham, Utah, was a man with a mission. In 1916, admirers of John Wesley Powell had erected a monument at the South Rim of the Grand Canyon honoring the Major's pioneering river journeys. Omitted from the monument, however, were the names of O. W. Howland, Seneca Howland, and Bill Dunn, who had left the first Powell expedition at Separation Canyon in 1869. These three men were "deserters," the reasoning went, but Frazier didn't think so. To correct this injustice, he decided to place a plaque commemorating the three men at Separation Canyon. Frazier recruited his friend and fellow river runner, Frank Swain; Frank's cousins Bus and Alton Hatch; Royce Mowrey, the Hatch's brother-in-law; Bill Fahrni, a friend from Lark, Utah, and Clyde Eddy, the well-known author and river runner. Eddy, with his own agenda, hired cameraman Fred Jayne to record the trip—the dream of a commercial film, like the lure of gold, has always been around. The river was the lowest it had been in years, and the run was brutally hard. Rapids were impassable gardens of exposed boulders; it was cruelly hot, the water was little more than thin mud. Tensions ran high, as they always do on such a trip, but

they finally won through, and in only eighteen days. In due course they reached Separation Canyon and mounted the plaque, a simple copper sheet with the names and dates punched in by Bus Hatch. The three "deserters" had finally received their due. The Dusty Dozen continued on to the site of Boulder Dam, where they still had enough spirit to ask the engineer in charge if they could run their boats through the diversion tunnel. Unfortunately, Frazier had not correctly figured the level of Lake Mead, and the rising waters covered the plaque. In 1939, he motored up Lake Mead with Julius Stone and placed another marker higher up, but within a few years it too was threatened. It wasn't until 1943 that the present cenotaph was finally mounted far enough above the reservoir level to be safe.

The Stone-Frazier Party in Glen Canyon, 1938

In 1937, Dr. Russell Frazier and his friend Charles Kelly took a motorboat up Glen Canyon from Lees Ferry to look for the "Spanish steps," reportedly the site where the Franciscans Domínguez and Escalante had chopped steps in the sandstone to get their horses down into Glen Canyon. Known as "El Vado de los Padres," Crossing of the Fathers, the site was

actually known to experienced canyoneers; Dave Rust had visited it as recently as 1925. But Frazier and Kelly decided that they had "rediscovered" the site and that furthermore it was of such significance that it merited a commemorative plaque to mark the spot. The next year Frazier organized an expedition to return to the spot and do just that. Besides Kelly and Frazier, the party included Doc Inglesby, Julius Stone, his son George Stone, and Bill Cryst. Frank Swain was in charge of the boats. Stone, even though he was eighty-three years old, jumped at the chance to return to Glen Canyon, where he had many happy memories and some not so pleasant. The party got on the river at Hite and motored all the way up to the last rapid in Cataract Canyon before floating down to the site of the crossing. There with appropriate ceremony they affixed a copper plaque to the canyon wall near the site. Their duty done, they continued downstream. As they floated past the wreck of the Hoskaninni dredge, they stopped to explore the ruin and salvage some timbers for that night's campfire. Standing by the fire that night, Stone looked into his coffee cup and reflected that the coffee was the only return he ever got from his investment in the Hoskaninni Mining Company. "This cup of coffee," he mused, "cost me $5,000."

Haldane "Buzz" Holmstrom with Lois Jotter, 1938

By 1937, when Buzz Holmstrom decided to float the Green and Colorado rivers, he had already been down the Rogue River in Oregon and the Salmon River in Idaho. The Colorado would be different, he figured, so he built his own boat out of native cedar from Oregon. He was planning to go with a friend who backed out at the last minute, but Buzz refused to give up his dream. If there was no one to go with, fine, he would go alone. He started from Green River, Wyoming, in September 1937 and took his time floating down the upper Green, reasoning that he was on the river to see how far he could get, not how many rapids he could run, nor how fast he could make the trip. He didn't want to risk wrecking his boat, but as he gained confidence, he ran more and more rapids that were usually portaged, drifting into them with a chew of tobacco in his cheek, singing "Barnacle Bill the Sailor." He portaged only four rapids the entire time, partly because he didn't want to carry all his equipment around the falls. When Buzz reached Lake Mead after the first, and one of the only, solo traverses of the canyons, he refused the offer of a tow across the reservoir from a Park Service motorboat. After soloing all the way, he wanted to finish the last leg of the trip in the same fashion. He rowed for three days across the still waters, and on Thanksgiving Day 1937, bumped the bow of his boat against the massive wall of the dam. When this picture was taken, Buzz was working for the Bureau of Reclamation in Marble Canyon, and had taken time off to meet the Nevills Expedition (including Lois Jotter, one of the crew) as they rested and prepared for their journey through the Grand Canyon. After a trip in 1938 with Amos Burg, and a few odd jobs with the U.S.G.S., Buzz was restless. Just before World War II, an adventuresome widow named Mrs. Clegg hired him to fulfill a dream of journeying across North America from British Columbia by boat. Amazingly enough, they made it, reaching New York City just as World War II broke out. Buzz served in the Navy after America entered the war, contracted malaria, and left the service shortly after the war ended. He returned to the river, guiding survey parties from the Bureau of Reclamation on the Grande Ronde river in eastern Oregon. One spring day in May, 1946 Buzz borrowed a rifle from the camp cook, saying he was "going to shoot a chicken." A short while later, the men heard a shot and found Buzz dead of a gunshot wound in the head. It was a sad end for one of the Colorado's foremost rivermen.

The "French Trio," 1938

Bernard DeColmont was the only experienced kayaker among the trio when they decided to attempt the Colorado in 1938. Bernard was associated with the Paris Museum of Natural History, and had only recently married Genevieve. Antoine DeSeyne (left) was a neighbor and skiing partner of Bernard's. Their avowed purpose in coming all the way from France was to try the "equipment and techniques they use in running the waters in Europe [on] the most wonderful river in the world." Each of the French adventurers piloted their own fifteen-foot kayak down the river. They started in southern Wyoming, below the town of Green River, in September of 1938. They reached Jensen, Utah, some 300 miles downstream, the first week of October. There they were treated to all the hospitality that Jensen and nearby Vernal could provide—Frenchmen, and especially attractive young French women, were a rarity in eastern Utah at the time. During their layover in Vernal, they stayed with local riverman Bus Hatch and his family. Though they planned to go all the way through the Grand Canyon, floating ice in Glen Canyon and continued cold weather caused them to postpone and finally cancel the rest of their trip. They left the river at Lees Ferry and returned to France. Genevieve DeColmont was the first, and indeed for many years the only, woman to pilot her own boat down the river. Toward the end of the their journey, in Cataract Canyon, they stopped to add their name to a river register high up on the canyon wall. "[I]nstinctively, naturally, and without thinking," Antoine DeSeyne later wrote, "we wrote our collective name, the name of the team, the 'French Trio.' It was a team that had gotten that far, a French team, and that was enough."

Barry Goldwater at the Utah-Arizona Border, Glen Canyon, 1940

In 1940 Barry Goldwater, future senator from Arizona, set out to fulfill a "lifetime ambition to explore by boat the Green and Colorado Rivers." Although he had been planning to go with Norm Nevills for nearly a year, he almost didn't make it. His wife and mother-in-law were strongly opposed to his risking his life for such a foolhardy reason, and almost talked him out of it. Displaying the talents that would make him a master politician in later years, he reached a compromise. The party was actually starting in Green River, Wyoming; he would join them in Green River, Utah, and only run Cataract and Grand Canyons. One factor that won over Mrs. Goldwater was the fact that the party included two women: Mildred Baker, and Nevills' wife Doris. They were, incidentally, the first, and some of the only women to ever run the rivers all the way from Wyoming to Lake Mead. In three of Nevills' cataract boats, the party made good time, despite hanging up on rocks in Cataract Canyon. On August 1st, just above Lees Ferry, they crossed into Goldwater's "beloved Arizona." To commemorate the occasion, Goldwater chiseled "ARIZONA WELCOMES YOU" on a canyon wall where it was visible from the river. He noted in his diary: "I noticed immediately a more bracing quality in the air; a clearer, bluer sky, a more buoyant note in the song of the birds; a snap and sparkle in the air that only Arizona air has, and I said to myself, without reference to a map, that we were now HOME."

Nevills Expeditions, Grand Canyon, 1941

Agnes Albert (center) was the wife of a diplomat, living on Nob Hill in San Francisco, when she heard of Nevills Expeditions. Distressed by the course of events in Europe, where her family lived, she contacted Nevills and asked if she could accompany his 1941 Grand Canyon expedition. Sure, Norm told her. More than any other person of his day, Norm Nevills saw the future of river running as a tourist business for everyone, not a guide service for explorers. He was the first to take women on river trips in the Grand Canyon, Cataract Canyon, and elsewhere, and took anyone, regardless of age, sex, or previous experience, on his San Juan River trips. Nevills ran essentially two kinds of river trips. Each year he would plan a major trip, usually the Grand Canyon or the Green River, although in 1946 he ran the Snake and Salmon in Idaho. These trips were expensive—as much as $2,000—and long, usually lasting at least a month. For the rest of the season, from April to September or even later

if there was enough water, he would run ten-day trips on the San Juan River, floating from his home at Mexican Hat to Lees Ferry. The San Juan run was his "bread and butter" trip; he used the proceeds from those to finance his Grand Canyon tours. When he started out, he charged $75 for the trip, which had risen to $200 by the time he died in 1949. Still, it was the Grand Canyon that Nevills always came back to. Of the first one hundred people through the canyon, almost half went with Nevills Expeditions. Others in the photo are, left to right: Zee Grant, the kayaker; Nevills; Agnes Albert; Bill Schukraft; Del Reid, a boatman for Nevills on several of his early trips; and Weldon Heald, a well-known photographer. The boat is named for Nevills' father, William E. Nevills.

Louis West Marooned at Separation Canyon, 1940

In the summer of 1940, river-rat Harry Aleson convinced a friend, Louis West, that they should motor up Lake Mead to the upper end and meet the Nevills Expedition at Separation Canyon. Nevills would be at the end of his second trip through the Grand Canyon, and Aleson planned to tow his boats across the shallows of Lake Mead, saving Norm and his tired boatmen the long pull across the still waters. While Aleson and West were waiting at Separation Canyon, they decided to see if they could retrace the route followed by the ill-fated members of the Powell party in 1869. After a long and hot hike—seventeen miles one way—they were stopped by an impassable cliff. On their return to the river, Aleson discovered to his dismay that his boat had come loose and disappeared downriver. Now the rescuers were perforce in the position of having to be rescued. To attract Nevills' attention, they hung a life jacket on a pair of crossed oars. Aleson then hiked up the river to the top of the rapid, which was all but covered by Lake Mead. There he stuck a driftwood branch in a ledge overhanging the river and attached his long underwear, by way of further signal. He then floated back to where Louis West was waiting. When Nevills reached Separation Rapid, he saw the signal, and found a note that Aleson had left describing their predicament. The river runners picked up their would-be benefactors and found Aleson's boat a few miles downstream. Then he kept his original intention; that night, as the boatmen slept on their boats, Aleson towed all four boats across miles of open water to safety, navigating across the dark lake by dead reckoning.

Alexander "Zee" Grant in the Grand Canyon, 1941

In the fall of 1938, a young man from Salt Lake City named Stewart Gardiner ran his folding kayak through the canyons of the upper Green. The next year, he made the same trip, only this time with Alexander Grant, better known as Zee. Grant was an experienced kayaker and a member of the Explorer's Club. In 1941, Grant heard that Norm Nevills was planning to take a small party through the Grand Canyon and immediately wrote Nevills asking to come along. Reluctant at first, Nevills finally agreed, although not without misgivings. Grant's *Escalante* was a larger version of the standard folding kayak available at the time. For flotation, he used inner tubes as sponsons, or side stabilizers, and stuffed the inside of the kayak with brightly colored beachballs. Nevills fears seemed justified when Grant miscalculated in Badger, the first major rapid in the Grand Canyon, and was thrown from his kayak. But he caught up, climbed aboard, and paddled through the tailwaves sitting backwards on top of the *Escalante*. Not to be outdone, Nevills later on went through a small rapid standing on his head on the deck of the kayak while Agnes Albert, the only woman on the trip, paddled. Grant ran most of the rapids in the Grand Canyon, portaging only major cataracts like

Lava Falls. He was the first person to run a kayak through the Grand Canyon. Grant later went on to help found the American Whitewater Affiliation and run many other American rivers. Note the many patches on the canvas hull of the *Escalante* that are visible in this photograph.

Georgie White and Harry Aleson, Lower Grand Canyon, 1945

When Georgie White and Harry Aleson met in Los Angeles in 1944, Georgie's young daughter had just been killed in a bicycle accident. Georgie was despondent, and when the grieving Georgie met the restless Aleson, something clicked. In August of that year, Georgie, Harry, and a young biologist from the Los Angeles City College climbed out of the Grand Canyon and trudged across the desolate Arizona Strip. During that long, hot walk, they fell to discussing how to get a stranded river party out of the canyon. It was obvious that walking out wasn't the answer. Why not float out, using life jackets equipped with waterproof survival kits? Determined to give the idea a try, Georgie and Harry hiked into the Grand Canyon from Peach Springs in June 1945, worked their way sixty miles upriver along the banks, tightened their jackets, and stepped out into the current wearing Mae West life jackets, swimming suits, and tennis shoes. Gripping each other's wrists, they careened downstream, and were sucked into whirlpools, scraped over rocks, threatened by floating logs. Bruised and waterlogged by the time they reached Lake Mead, they were nevertheless ready to try it again the next year, and this time from farther upstream. The second time, after futile attempts to build a raft from driftwood, they rode downstream in a six-foot Navy survival raft. The little raft was tossed like a leaf in the turbulent rapids, but again they made it safely through. Although they took trips together after their second Grand Canyon adventure, from then on they were in more conventional craft.

Willie Taylor at Jensen, Utah, 1947
Plaque and Inscription Marking Willie's Grave, Marble Canyon

Wilson Taylor was a resident of southern California and a friend of Otis "Dock" Marston. Marston introduced Willie to Norm Nevills, and Willie signed on as a passenger on Nevills's 1947 run of the Green River. After that trip Willie couldn't get enough of river running. The next year, he went along with Marston in an attempt to run a powerboat, Ed Hudson's *Esmerelda II*, upstream into the Grand Canyon. The effort failed, but the same crew tried again in 1949 and 1950, recording the first powerboat runs of the canyon, and getting a little farther upstream each time. The usual procedure was to run the boats downstream, caching gasoline and food at various places in the canyon for the upriver run. On the third downstream run, Hudson crashed the ESMERELDA II into a rock along the shore, throwing Taylor from the boat. Marston, driving a Chris-Craft inboard, came to his rescue, and threw him a rope. Taylor, meanwhile, had gotten tangled with a stray rope from Hudson's boat, and then the two ropes became ensnared, one of them looping around Taylor's neck. Marston, trying to avoid trouble with his boat, powered back upstream and almost choked Willie to death dragging him underwater.

Undeterred by his close call in 1950, Willie Taylor returned for a more conventional downriver trip with Marston in 1956. By then Willie was older and in ill health. On the third day of the trip, at Mile 44 in Marble Canyon, Taylor suffered a fatal heart attack in camp. His friends buried him then and there, much to the consternation of the National Park Service. The next year Marston returned and marked the grave with a memorial plaque. Nearby lies Peter Hansborough, who drowned on the Brown-Stanton expedition in 1889.

Ed Hudson on the *Esmerelda II*, 1949

Ed Hudson, a pharmacist from Paso Robles, California, was a man with a dream: he wanted to be the first person to ever run a powerboat up the Grand Canyon. He floated the Colorado with Norm Nevills in 1942 to reconnoiter, and on the trip met Otis Marston, who would later also become obsessed with the idea of the upriver run. By 1948, Hudson was ready to try to realize his ambition. He had a special boat, which he called the *Esmerelda II*, built in Seattle for the attempt. Hiring Marston as a guide, he started from Lake Mead in June. They barely made it into the lower Grand Canyon, however, and Hudson vowed to try again the next year with a more powerful engine. At Marston's suggestion, they first ran downriver, checking the rapids and stashing fuel and supplies for the upriver run as they went. On the upstream try, they got a few miles farther, but high water defeated them once again. In 1950 Hudson made his third and final try. This time Marston was in his own boat, a

Chris-Craft with an inboard motor. Hudson ran most of the major rapids down to the Hermit Trail successfully, but lost control in Tuna Creek Rapid, about Mile 100, and the *Esmerelda II* crashed into the rocks. The party gathered on shore to survey the damage to Hudson's boat. Despairing of ever realizing his dream (and some say, secretly relieved), Hudson untied the stricken craft and, in an emotional scene, committed it to the river. The *Esmerelda II* was made of sturdier stuff, however, and didn't sink. It was found later by the Rigg brothers, Bob and Jim, who patched it together and brought it out to Lake Mead. There Hudson found out about it, and claimed it was still his property; the Rigg brothers claimed right of salvage. There was a great amount of haggling and threatened lawsuits, and the boat was finally donated to Grand Canyon National Park, where it is still on display at the South Rim Visitors Center.

John and Leo Krusack at Lees Ferry, 1952

Until the end of World War II, Glen Canyon and the San Juan River were well known only to prospectors, Indians, and a handful of river runners like Dave Rust and Norm Nevills. Both had been taking tourists down the canyons for a number of years, but the numbers were limited by the type of boats each used: Rust, folding canoes, and Nevills, wooden "San Juan punts," as he called them. Very few individuals went on their own without benefit of either of these men as their guide. The end of the war, however, brought cheap, easily obtainable rafts, plentiful gasoline, and increasing hordes of tourists into the remote canyons of the Colorado. When a film about Nevills' trips on the San Juan, *Danger River*, won an Academy Award in 1947, Glen Canyon and the San Juan river were, once again, "discovered." There was yet another rush to the canyons, but this time it was to float the rivers. Within a decade of the premier of *Danger River*, a dozen outfitters offered trips down both rivers. Whole troops of Boy Scouts floated down, along with church groups, geologists, honeymooners, and little old ladies. Many tourists now chose to go on their own; one of the beauties of Glen Canyon, at least, was that you could make it without a guide. The Krusack brothers of Illinois were two such independent tourists. They wrote to Norm Nevills asking his advice, and when he assured them they could do it, ran the San Juan and Glen Canyon in

two foldboats and an inflatable raft. The boom in tourism reached its peak during the construction of Glen Canyon Dam, as thousands rushed to see the beauties of the canyons before they were covered forever by Lake Powell.

Bill Beer and John Daggett at Lake Mead, April 1955

Bill Beer and his friend, John Daggett, were life-insurance salesman from southern California. They must not have seemed like good risks, though, when they decided to try something unique for their vacation in 1955. Although many river runners had floated rapids in life jackets, it was usually inadvertent, the result of being tossed from a boat. Daggett and Beer decided to do it on purpose—to float the entire length of the Grand Canyon using only life jackets and waterproof boxes to hold them up. After much careful planning, the daring duo left Lees Ferry on April 10th, wearing surplus wet-suit tops, swim fins, and long underwear, with their provisions and gear stowed in two large, black rubber waterproof radio boxes each. At first they let the boxes float free, attached to their wrists with a long cord. After John Daggett was almost drowned when the boxes went on one side of a boulder and he on the other, however, they held the boxes under their arms and floated on them. Although they made an effort to pick out routes through the rapids, they were really completely at the mercy of the Colorado. The water was chilly (although not as cold as today), and they were often sucked under by whirlpools or scraped over rocks, but amazingly enough, both men reached Lake Mead, little the worse for their trip. Their record remained unchallenged—much to the relief of the National Park Service—until 1988, when a German adventurer named Werner Kraus swam the entire river, duplicating their voyage. Kraus,

however, was wearing a state-of-the-art flotation suit and was supported by a boat from Hatch River Expeditions. It's doubtful that anyone will ever truly duplicate what Bill Beer called "a cheap vacation that got out of hand."

The End of the First "Friendship Cruise" Near Moab, Utah, 1957

The Friendship Cruise was first organized by the chambers of commerce of Moab and Green River, Utah. For an entrance fee, boaters were provided with gas, rest stops, and search and rescue service. Two years later, in 1959, over four hundred boats signed up for the trip. Around the same time, as Lake Powell began to fill, citizens of Moab proposed using nuclear explosives to blow the rapids out of Cataract Canyon so the Friendship Cruisers could motor right into Lake Powell. Fortunately, this plan was never taken seriously. A highlight of the Friendship Cruise was a massive steak fry and dance held *al fresco* at Anderson Bottom on the lower Green River. The cruise was usually held on Memorial Day weekend, when both rivers were at their highest stages, making powerboat runs feasible. Boaters would start in Green River, Utah, go down the Green for 120 miles, and then go up the Colorado for about 50 miles to a landing below Moab. For many years, a marathon race was held as part of the festivities; the fastest time, just under three hours to make the 180-mile trip, was recorded in 1966 by a boater from Grand Junction, Colorado. In later years, the event was marred by several deaths. Two men drowned when they made a wrong turn at the confluence and their boat was destroyed in Cataract Canyon. Later, another entrant lost his life when his boat overturned while trying to negotiate the Slide, a small rapid on the Colorado. High gasoline prices in the 1970s, and low water in the 1980s, forced the cancellation of the Friendship Cruise many times during the decade, but under the right conditions it is still a popular event on the river.

Walter Kirschbaum

By 1960, private river runners in many different types of craft were becoming fairly common on the Green and the Colorado Rivers; there were cataract boats, Galloway boats, ten-man rafts, pontoons, varieties of dories and other home-built designs. Kayaks, however, were still uncommon. Kayakers were looked on as "gamblers" and "screwballs" if not downright suicidal. The problem was the size of the boat. People looked at the little, seemingly frail craft and shook their heads. The bigger the boat the safer the ride, right?

Not necessarily true, as kayakers have always known to their delight. Although there were a few kayaks down the Green in the 1930s, the first to take one down the Grand Canyon was "Zee" Grant in 1941. And even then he portaged some of the biggest rapids. The first to run all the rapids in the Grand in a kayak was Walter Kirschbaum, a champion kayak racer from Salida, Colorado. Originally from Germany, Kirschbaum learned his *wildwasser* ("wild water") skills from one of the great German kayakers, Theo Bock. Drafted into the German army, Kirschbaum fought on the eastern front and lived through a Russian prison camp, being released in 1946. By the time he came to the U.S. to race in Salida, Colorado, in 1955, he had already run all the "canyons of reputation" in the old country. Kirschbaum swept the national and international kayak championships with his marvelous paddling skill, but something in him changed at the same time. As he wrote, "I began to enjoy exploring remote rivers more than racing. I found wilderness canyons so attractive that all the success I had had in races of national and international level faded in importance."

By 1959 Kirschbaum was ready to tackle what he called the "Problem trip"—the Grand Canyon. The Park Service wasn't ready to let him, however, and denied Kirschbaum a permit. With the help of attorney Tyson Dines, another avid and adventurous river runner of

those days, he was finally allowed to go, provided he first successfully run Cataract Canyon and other difficult stretches of whitewater. This he did, and was finally judged ready to attempt the Grand the next year, 1960. He left Lees Ferry in his 16-foot, hand-built fiberglass and canvas kayak, on about 40,000 cubic feet of water. He was accompanied by Tyson Dines (in a 23-foot Canadian freight canoe with an outboard motor!) and Ted Hatch, of Hatch River Expeditions, who was running a motorized pontoon with six "selected passengers." Kirschbaum's only serious upset came in Hance Rapid—that graveyard of reputations—where a "giant's fist" rolled him over, tore his paddle from his hands, and dragged him out of his kayak. Regaining his capsized boat, Kirschbaum calmly climbed aboard the hull, reached under to his spare paddle, assembled it, and then paddled to shore.

The rest of the trip was easy in comparison, even Lava Falls, where his greatest thrill was watching Georgie White take a boatload of dudes through the worst part of the rapid; one of the three pontoons in her triple-rig heeled over to past vertical, almost creating a "Georgie sandwich," but the rigging snapped the pontoon back to its normal position, without throwing anyone out. Just another run of Lava for Georgie, but Kirschbaum noted that "this was the greatest spectacle I had seen, and I must have screamed with fear, watching it from shore." Kirschbaum's party reached Temple Bar on Lake Mead after paddling over 300 miles in six days, and Walter Kirschbaum entered the pages of history.

Jon Hamilton in Lava Falls, 1960

Driving a boat "against the grain"—upstream—through the Grand Canyon was the dream of a number of individuals since the late 1930s. First to try was Harry Aleson, with his grandly styled Colorado Up River Expedition. Next was Ed Hudson, whose *Esmerelda II* wasn't up to the rigors of the river and was finally abandoned in mid-canyon. In 1959, another party decided to try to make the up-run, this time using special jet boats manufactured by Indiana Gear Works and based on a New Zealand design. Piloting the boats was Jon Hamilton, son of the New Zealand inventor of the boats, and Bill Austin, who had secured the rights for the Indiana company. Despite the powerful engines, the 1959 run failed to get even as far up-river as Aleson had gotten with his puny outboards. In 1960, they tried again, this time with Dock Marston as chief navigator. By now a down-river run before attempting the up-run had become traditional, so that they could check water levels and stash gas and other supplies. After a false start, the down run went fine until Lava Falls, where the boat piloted by Bill Austin took flight on top of a wave and came down hard, fracturing Austin's leg badly; he was evacuated by helicopter. The rest of the party continued to Boulder City, overhauled the boats (the *Wee Red*, the *Wee Yellow*, the *Dock*, and the *Kiwi*) and began their up-run attempt on July 6th. As expected, the major obstacle was at Lava Falls. After a number of attempts, Jon Hamilton was able to get all four boats over the falls and they proceeded upriver. Not without problems, however; Dock Marston strained his shoulder, crewman Ed I'Anson cracked four ribs, and the boats took a terrible pounding, necessitating constant stops for repairs. Still, they were able to push upstream and reach Phantom Ranch about a week after they started. Don Neff, at the time a boatman for a Mexican Hat Expeditions trip that was camped at Bright Angel Creek, remembered that after the four boats roared into the beach the members of the up-run crew were cocky and sure their trip was almost over. The next day, however, in attempting Grapevine Rapid, the *Wee Yellow* hit a wave so hard that the weakened deck was torn from the boat; she sank at once. The driver was rescued but many tools, cameras, personal items, and worst of all, exposed film, was irretrievably lost. Neff recalls a much humbled bunch of jet-boaters that crept back to Phantom Ranch that night. More carefully now, the up-runners were able to push their boats all the way to Lees Ferry. The first up-run was ironically the last; dismayed by the noise and danger, and responding to numerous complaints, the National Park Service promptly banned any future up-runs.

CHAPTER 5
Outfitters

The first time, I guess it was simply running away from where my parents lived. Me and them didn't get along too well. And then once I got down into the canyons, it felt like a place I could do better in. It felt more like home, down here, I suppose. Seemed like I knew all about old Bert Loper the minute I first saw him sitting on that rock below Red Canyon riffle with no clothes on . . . turning red in the sun. And he knew right away that I knew. We were just old brothers that hadn't met til then. I don't think I ever came into the canyons as a visitor. I wasn't a tourist. I was always just coming home.

—Bundy McKay, *Requiem for a River Rat*

There's an old saying, often applied to commercial river runners, that compares them to the oldest profession. "First you do it for fun, then you do it for your friends, then you do it for money." Of course that could be applied to anything; but if the term "commercial river runner" is strictly defined as one who runs rivers for pay, then the earliest ones on the Colorado would have to be General Ashley's nervous trappers or Major Powell's contentious crew. Nathaniel Galloway, Bert Loper, and Dave Rust all acted as guides and boatmen for river parties as early as 1900. As the term is generally understood today, and on the scale practiced today, the first commercial river runners got their start on the Green and the Colorado in the 1930s. It is safe to say that without exception all commercial outfitters began their careers on the water as a private individuals looking for a way to finance their own passion—running rivers.

Like so many good ideas, it seems that several people came up with the idea of herding passengers down the river for pay at about the same time. One was Bus Hatch of Vernal, Utah. Bus and his cousin Frank Swain learned the basics of boats and river from Parley Galloway, Nathaniel's son. The two novices started running the upper Green for excitement in 1932; later, Bus began to take an occasional passenger along to help share expenses, and gradually it grew into a business. During the hard years of the Depression, however, the business remained little more than a dream.

Meanwhile, Norman Nevills of Mexican Hat, Utah, took his first passengers down the San

Juan River in 1936. Although the weather turned bad and they ran out of food before the end of the trip, Nevills wasn't discouraged. In 1938 and again in 1940, he guided well-publicized parties down the Green and Colorado, parties that included a number of women. Bolstered by the publicity he received, Nevills had no trouble signing up passengers for his yearly runs of the Grand Canyon as well as trips on the Green, San Juan, other sections of the Colorado, and the Snake and Salmon rivers of Idaho. By the time that Nevills and his wife Doris were killed in a tragic plane crash in September, 1949 Nevills Expeditions was perhaps the best-known and most successful outfitter on the Colorado River.

Bus Hatch, however, was not far behind. He was still taking customers down the river, and, more important, sensed coming changes in river running as a business and responded accordingly. Nevills, until near the end of his life, dismissed inflatable boats as a fad, even though a raft could carry twice as many passengers as a cataract boat. Bus Hatch, along with son Don, was quick to realize that with inflatable rafts they could carry larger numbers of passengers and make river running a viable business.

What really put Hatch River Expeditions on a solid footing was the Echo Park Dam controversy, which began in the late 1940s and flared up off and on for the next ten years. In their efforts to stop construction of the dam, the Sierra Club and allied conservation groups sponsored river trips down the Green and the Yampa rivers to make public the beauty of the river canyons and to demonstrate that river running was a sport that could be enjoyed by anyone, not just daredevils, as the dam's supporters claimed. The person they chose to take these

"consciousness-raising" groups down the river was Bus Hatch. The resulting exposure boosted Hatch to a position in the national spotlight that Nevills, ever a publicity hound, would have envied.

Just a few years later, the same thing happened in Glen Canyon, as thousands flocked to see the wonders that were doomed by Lake Powell. By 1960, a dozen outfitters offered trips through Glen Canyon. Many of these were established businesses, others were church groups, clubs, or just share-the-expense groups with a common interest in river running. While the publicity turned river running into a thriving business, it also fostered competition. The 1950s could honestly be called the "Golden Age" of commercial river running. If someone wanted to start a river-running business, all that was needed was a couple of boats and some passengers. No rules, no regulations, no permits, just get in the boat and go. For passengers, the trips were cheap ($150 for a ten-day Grand Canyon trip, for instance), and there was still a spirit of adventure that is sometimes lacking today. The '50s saw the rapid growth of some established river outfits and the creation of new ones.

The first inflatable craft used were seven- and ten-man assault rafts. Later, as more and more people became interested in running rivers, bigger and bigger inflatables were used. Around the mid-1950s, a number of different people began to use bridge pontoons as a way of taking more customers down the rivers. No one knows just who was first to try the giant pontoons—up to thirty-eight feet long and ten feet wide—but by the end of the 1950s they were in common use. Bus Hatch used them up on the Green to carry huge Sierra Club groups at the same time Georgie White was trying them out in the Grand Canyon. At first they were propelled by two sets of oars, but this soon proved impractical, since a loaded pontoon could weigh as much as five tons, and if it filled with water in a rapid, many times that. Experimentation went on throughout the decade. First the rubber floors were cut out and replaced with suspended floors. Then the oars were supplemented by outboard motors. The outboards of the day were not waterproof, and would drown out in a rapid, so procedure called for securing the motor at the head of a big rapid and using the oars. Any honest boatman would admit, however, that the oars were useless and that the boat was essentially out of control. At first the outboards were mounted to a frame off the stern of the boat, called a "tail-dragger." This made the boat turn quickly but left the motor unprotected from waves and rocks, and more than one outboard was lost off the back. Later the motor was mounted inside the boat, and a mounting called a "jackass" was developed that allowed the boatman to lever the motor out of the water if threatened by rocks in shallow water.

One established outfit that stayed on the river was Norm Nevills' old company. After his death, it was taken over by two former boatmen, Jim Rigg and Frank Wright, and renamed Mexican Hat Expeditions. Rigg later sold out to Wright, who then took on a new partner, Gaylord Staveley, who had married Joan Nevills, one of Norm's daughters. About 1958, Wright sold his interest in the company so that he could go to work for the Glen Canyon Salvage Survey, just then getting under way. Under Staveley's guidance, Mexican Hat Expeditions made the essential change to inflatable boats

and evolved into Canyoneers, Inc., which is still in business.

Some of the other outfitters who got their start during the same period included Reynolds-Hallacy Expeditions, who ran trips on the upper Green; Harris-Brennan Expeditions, co-owned by Don Harris, another former Nevills boatman; P. T. Reilly, who also started with Nevills, but later ran boats of his own design; Georgie White, the first woman outfitter; Larabee-Aleson Western River Tours, run by that old river rat, Harry Aleson; and John Cross, who got his start shepherding groups of Boy Scouts through Glen Canyon. Still another was Jack Curry, who sued Hatch River Expeditions, claiming they had an unfair monopoly—Hatch had the only Park Service-issued permit, or concession, to operate in Dinosaur National Monument at the time—and won, getting the right to take passengers through the canyons of the Green and Colorado. Curry's Western River Expeditions (now in different hands) is one of the largest river outfitters in business today.

There were others, but the happy situation that the early outfitters had enjoyed was about to change for good. Government agencies, from the Public Utilities Commission of Utah to the National Park Service to the U.S. Coast Guard took notice of the increased activity on the Green and the Colorado and decided that the free and easy days of the outfitters were over. The agencies started requiring licenses for boatmen and companies; insurance policies; limits on sizes of groups and type and size of boats; permits to float the rivers; and quotas on the number of outfitters allowed to use a certain stretch of river.

The restrictions imposed by the government, however irritating to the old-timers, didn't really curtail the number of people who signed on as passengers on commercial river trips. If anything, they actually helped the outfitters by providing a patina of official respectability—"licensed guides" and "official concessionaire" became selling points—and by restricting the numbers of permits given to private individuals. By the beginning of the 1960s, a number of commercial river outfitters, tested in the free-market days of the previous decade, and with established reputations, stood poised for the great boom in outdoor recreation that was to begin before the decade was over.

David Dexter Rust at the Bright Angel Tramway, 1903

David Dexter Rust is one of the least known but most interesting figures in river-running history. A native of Kanab, Utah, he was a graduate of Brigham Young Academy and Stanford University, served in both houses of the Utah legislature, and was superintendent of schools for Kane County for three terms. In 1903, he established Rust's Camp, now Phantom Ranch, in the Grand Canyon and built the first aerial tramway, or cable car, across the Colorado River at the mouth of Bright Angel creek. After Rust's Camp was bought out by Fred Harvey, Rust became the manager of the Grand Canyon Transportation Company, working in the canyon from 1909 to 1915. During that time he guided such luminaries as Zane Grey, Theodore Roosevelt, John Burroughs, and John Muir on trips around the Grand Canyon. He was friends with many of the early river travelers, including Nathaniel Galloway, Julius Stone, the Kolb brothers, and Bert Loper. Around that same time, he bought some collapsible canvas canoes from the Kalamazoo Canvas Boat Company and went into business as a river outfitter in Glen Canyon. Many early river travelers comment on the depth and breadth of Rust's knowledge of the canyons; Emery Kolb remembered that Rust had waited for him and Ellsworth at Lees Ferry in 1911 to tell them about the rapids to come and to warn them not to try to run Soap Creek. Ignoring his advice, Ellsworth flipped both boats. An extremely well-read and literate man, Rust often quoted Thoreau, Charles Lummis, and other nature philosophers. Rust himself was far ahead of his time in viewing tourism as a business, and took his own traveling quite seriously. "A thorough traveler," he wrote, " must be something of a geologist, something of a botanist, an archaeologist, an ornithologist, an artist, a philosopher, and so on. Through it all he is likely to be friendly with a camera. He must be agreeable in society, contented in solitude, enthusiastic and patient as a fisherman." Finally, he noted, quoting Thoreau, "traveling is no mere pastime." Rust died in 1963, as the final touches were being put on Glen Canyon Dam, which would alter his beloved canyon country forever.

The Stern-Wheeler *Cliff Dweller*, 1905

The *Cliff Dweller* was one of the largest craft ever to float on the upper Colorado. Steamboats of her size were common below the Grand Canyon, but for the upper Green River, she was unprecedented. She started life as the *City of Moab* in 1905, built in Grand Junction, Colorado, at a cost of $15,000. The steamer was launched at Green River, Utah, in May of that year. The maiden voyage, down the Green and up the Colorado to Moab, didn't auger well for the *City of Moab*'s future as a passenger and pleasure craft. On the way downriver, she struck several sandbars with such force that members of the crew were pitched headlong into the river. On the way up the Colorado, the boat failed to negotiate the Slide, a small rapid not far above the confluence, and was ignominiously forced to head back up the Green. She was then dry-docked at the mouth of the San Rafael River, at Tom Wimmer's ranch. New engines were installed, the stern lengthened by ten feet to accommodate a new paddle wheel, and the craft was renamed *Cliff Dweller*. The modifications didn't make much difference, however, and the revamped steamer barely made the twenty-five miles back upriver to Green River. No further tries were made to navigate the unfriendly waters of the Green and the Colorado; shortly thereafter the boat was dismantled and shipped to Saltair, a resort on the Great Salt Lake. There the *Cliff Dweller*, neé *City of Moab* finally found a home. She was christened *Vista*, and took tourists for cruises on the Great Salt Lake for many years.

The Steamboat *Comet* on the Green River, 1908

Around the same time that rivermen like H. E. Blake, Tom Wimmer, and Edwin Wolverton were experimenting with powered boats on the lower Green and Colorado, their contemporaries on the upper Green River were having the same kinds of ideas. The Green near the little town of Green River, Wyoming, flows swift and calm, ideal, it would seem, for a steamboat line. There were many ranches strung up and down the river, and a steamboat could pay for itself by hauling freight and passengers between Green River (which was on the railroad) and the isolated ranch houses. Or so the reasoning went, anyway. The first on the river was a small powered launch named, patriotically, the *Teddy R.*, which was used for pleasure trips and picnics up and down the river. Also that same year, 1908, a much more ambitious craft was launched. This was the *Comet*, a stern-wheel steamboat that was sixty feet long with a twelve-foot beam. She was built by the Green River Navigation Company at a cost of $25,000. The plan was to haul freight and passengers between Green River and the little town of Linwood, which was the center of the many prosperous ranches in the Lucerne Valley, downstream about forty-five miles. Unfortunately, the Green is too shallow for most of the year for a boat of such deep draft, and after only a couple of trips, the *Comet* was tied up near Green River and abandoned. The final attempt at a larger than rowboat-sized craft was the *Sunbeam*, a gasoline- powered stern-wheeler. From 1908 to 1910, it was also used for pleasure trips on the river, until it broke down near Big Piney, Wyoming. From there, it was hauled overland to Fremont Lake, repaired and modified, and used for many more years.

Don and Bus Hatch on the Yampa, 1956

Bus Hatch is generally conceded to be the first river runner to make a living "piloting dudes" down the Green and Colorado rivers. He and his cousin, Frank Swain, learned boats and rivers from Parley Galloway. In 1929, Galloway was thrown in jail in Vernal, Utah, where Frank was a deputy sheriff. He told the cousins that if they would help him make his bail, he would show them how to build a boat and take them down the Green. They got him out, whereupon Parley skipped town and was seldom seen in Vernal again. The two had absorbed enough from him to give it a try on their own, though, and after a few unsuccessful ventures soon became good boatmen. Bus's early trips were mostly cost-sharing excursions during the hard times of the Depression. As his enterprise became known, how-

ever, people began to hire him as a guide. His business struggled at first, mainly because of the limitations of the wooden boat. Bus was a carpenter by trade, and made fine boats. They were good for running rivers, but could carry only two passengers at most, and then they had to cling to the decks like so much baggage. When surplus inflatable craft became widely available at the end of World War II, Bus's son Don convinced his father that here at last was a way to make a good living running rivers. His big break came in the late 1940s, when the public outcry over plans to build a dam in Dinosaur National Monument catapulted the Green River into the national headlines. As part of its campaign to defeat the dam, the Sierra Club sponsored trips down the Green and Yampa to show that river running was for everyone, not just fools and daredevils. As a guide the club hired the only person who could take large groups of people down the river, Bus Hatch. The resulting exposure made him the best known of the 1950s-era river outfitters. Bus's sons Gus, Don, Frank, and Ted were introduced to the river business at an early age—Don noted that he remembered riding in a Galloway boat when he was too small to see out of the cockpit. After Bus died in 1967, his sons continued in the business of "piloting dudes," and today they are still some of the largest river outfitters in the world.

Doris, Joan, and Norman Nevills, 1947

Norm Nevills was one of the other pioneers of commercial river running and the first to actively promote river running as a form of mass tourism. Legend has it that he took his new bride, Doris Drown, on their honeymoon trip down the San Juan in a boat made of boards salvaged from a horse trough and an outhouse. That was in 1934; he took his first paying passengers down the San Juan two years later. His first big break came in 1938, when he guided a scientific party from the University of Michigan through Cataract and Grand canyons. Included among the passengers were two women, botanist Dr. Elzada Clover and her assistant, Lois Jotter. They were the first women to run the Grand Canyon, and the resulting publicity ensured Nevills' fame. He designed and built his own boats, flat-bottomed skiffs he called cataract boats, based on plans he obtained from his father, who had been in the Yukon gold rush in 1898. Nevills's detractors called them sad-iron skiffs, from a resemblance to that common household tool. And detractors there were; Nevills was a showman, jealous of the spotlight, and resented anyone who took attention away from him. People either loved and adored him, like his family and many others, or hated him passionately, like Otis Marston, the river historian. There was little middle ground.

Nevills ran another well-publicized trip in 1940, this time from Wyoming all the way through the Grand Canyon. Besides his wife Doris, the crew included Mildred Baker, making them the first women to traverse the river from Wyoming to Arizona. Also along for part of the trip was Barry Goldwater, future senator from Arizona. To Nevills' credit, many commercial and private river runners got their start on a Nevills Expeditions trip. He was the first to see the tourist potential of running the Colorado through the Grand Canyon, at a time when most thought the Colorado all but impassable. And he pioneered in taking women on his trips, saying that they "made the best men." When she got old enough, Nevills also included his daughter Joan, who accompanied her father down the Green River in 1947 and the Grand Canyon in 1949, as well as on many trips on the San Juan. After surviving many runs of the Green, Colorado, and San Juan with no flips, indeed scarcely a scratch, Norman and Doris were killed when his airplane crashed just after takeoff at Mexican Hat, Utah, in September 1949. Joan later operated Mexican Hat Expeditions, the successor to Nevills Expeditions, for many years.

Harry Aleson and Ralph Badger at Hite, 1946

Harry Aleson was a true "river rat." As a soldier in World War I, he was gassed while in the trenches; as a consequence of that, he suffered from chronic stomach pains the rest of his life. The pain, or, as he liked to say, his Viking heritage, made him into a wanderer. In 1939, his loose feet led him to Lake Mead and the lower Grand Canyon. Harry promptly fell in love with the Colorado River and never strayed far from it for the rest of his life. After a number of frustrating attempts to run a motorboat up the Colorado, which he typically and grandly styled the COLORADO UP RIVER EXPEDITION, and his spectacular stunts of swimming the lower canyon with Georgie White, Harry turned to more conventional downriver journeys. A failed attempt at a partnership with Norm Nevills led to his starting a business with Charles Larabee—a bitter rival of Nevills—called Larabee-Aleson Western River Tours. With Larabee's financial backing, Aleson was finally able to make a living guiding tourists down the river. Aleson spent most of his time in Glen Canyon—such as this 1946 trip with

Ralph Badger, who had been on several trips with Nevills—although Aleson also ran the upper Green, Cataract Canyon, and occasionally the Grand Canyon. He was one of the pioneers in the use of inflatable rafts for river running, and Aleson's trips became known for the variety and quality of his meals—Aleson himself was often forced to live on baby food because of his bad stomach, and perhaps he developed a splendid river menu as a vicarious substitute.

Kent Frost Demonstrating His Skills as a Camp Cook at Lava Falls, 1947

Kent Frost started his river career after a stint in the Navy during World War II. Soon after being discharged, he signed on with Nevills as a boatman for a run through the Grand Canyon. Nevills was famous for hiring anyone, regardless of experience, as a boatman. When they came to rapids, Nevills would either run the boats through himself or would tell the fledgling—and nervous!—boatman, "Just follow me and do what I do." Frost had been on the San Juan with Nevills, and he was better prepared than most. Kent also acted as the cook for the trips, and so impressed the passengers with his culinary skills that, as he later commented, they wrote more about his cooking than about the canyon. Randall Henderson, the editor of *Desert* magazine and a passenger on the 1947 trip, bore this out: "He [Frost] doesn't bother with Coleman stoves and stone fireplaces. With a big frying pan, a couple of stew pans, a coffee pot and a pair of pliers to manipulate them, Kent would have the meal ready by the time the boats were unloaded and the bedrolls spread out for the night." Frost became one of Nevills' favorite boatmen, and made two more Grand Canyon trips with him as well as a number of trips on the San Juan River before Nevills was killed in 1949. In later years, Frost and his wife Fern started Kent Frost Canyonlands Jeep Tours, where he continued his exploratory and culinary traditions.

The Maiden Voyage of a Reynolds-Hallacy Cataract Boat on the Upper Green, 1947

In 1947, Norm Nevills returned to the upper Green River for a trip for the first time since 1940. Adrian Reynolds, the editor of the *Green River Star*, the local newspaper, was a man of some influence in the community, and helped Nevills with local arrangements for the trip, such as ensuring a sheriff's deputy would guard the boats at night and so on. He also made sure the trip was widely publicized, always appreciated by Nevills. Watching from the shore as Nevills pushed off was Reynolds' son, also named Adrian but known as A. K. A. K. was inspired by the call of the river and wrote to Nevills, asking for plans to build similar boats. Nevills wasn't normally one to encourage competition, but remembering the favors the senior Reynolds had done, he complied with the request. A. K. and friends Mike Hallacy and C. C. "Lug" Larsen each built a cataract boat to Nevills specifications, and went into business as Reynolds-Hallacy River Expeditions. They ran trips through the beautiful upper canyons

of the Green to Jensen, Utah, specializing mostly in charter groups of fishermen, hunters, or photographers. Their business ended when Flaming Gorge Dam was completed in 1963 and began flooding Flaming Gorge, Kingfisher, Horseshoe, and Red canyons. A. K. Reynolds, however, according to one story quit running the river when other outfitters began to use inflatable pontoons, saying that he didn't want to be on the same river as a "baloney boat."

John Cross on the First Explorer Scout Trip Through Glen Canyon, 1947

Soon after World War II, the Salt Lake City Council of the Boy Scouts began to think about a new outdoor adventure for its Explorer Scout program. It so happened that John Cross of Orem, Utah, a local scout leader, learned that the government was selling vast quantities of war materiel at a surplus center in Salt Lake City. Among the surplus items were inflatable life rafts and assault rafts. Cross and the other scout leaders got the idea of using the rafts to take Explorers on river trips through Glen Canyon. The scouts were required first to obtain all the necessary badges to reach Explorer status; the final requirement would be a trip through Glen Canyon. With $250 from the council, Cross was sent out to buy equipment. At first he thought about getting one-man life rafts for $1 each (complete with sail, paddles, emergency rations and water, and a distillation apparatus), but the image of dozens of scouts, each in his own raft, strung up and down the river gave him pause. He settled for ten seven-man rafts that cost $25 each. Thus began what was to become a tradition for Explorer Scouts for several years. The first trip took place in April 1947, with Bert Loper as the guide. (Harry Aleson was asked but said the river was too dangerous for scouts.) Later, as they gained experience, Cross began to lead the trips himself. After a couple of years, the Boy Scout council dropped the program. Cross, however, decided to go into the river-running business and started Cross Tours, which ran trips on the Grand Canyon and elsewhere until the late 1980s.

Moki-Mac—Malcolm Ellingson

Malcolm Ellingson worked at Hill Field, an Air Force base in northern Utah, in the late 1940s. He was also an enthusiastic local Boy Scout leader. Shortly after the war, when John

Cross and Albert Quist began taking scouts through Glen Canyon, Ellingson became involved and soon became the most vocal proponent of the trips. It was about the same time that he was given the name Moki-Mac, although no one seems to know just where the name came from. It stuck, however, and Moki-Mac became a fixture on Explorer Scout trips, famous for telling stories around the campfires. After the Boy Scout council dropped the program, Moki-Mac, John Cross, Al Quist, and other scout leaders continued taking groups of scouts down the river on their own. When the Quist brothers decided to start a commercial river-running business, they asked Ellingson if they could name it Moki-Mac Expeditions, since to a whole generation of Boy Scouts and their families the name symbolized river running. Later, Ellingson became the state park ranger at the Green River State Park in Green River, Utah. Moki-Mac was also a partner in the Quist family river-running business until his death.

Albert Quist on the Yampa, 1958

Albert Quist was a native of Salt Lake City, the descendant of Swedish immigrants who came to Utah in the nineteenth century as members of the L.D.S. (Mormon) church. (This Viking heritage was something he had in common with other Colorado rivermen, such as Harry Aleson, Buzz Holmstrom and Amos Burg.) In the years immediately following World War II, Quist worked for the Boy Scouts of America in Utah and Arizona and got involved with the Explorer Scout river-running program. He was along on the first trip, led by Bert Loper, and later guided trips on his own through Glen Canyon. After the program had been in existence for a few years, an editorial appeared in the *Deseret News*, a Salt Lake City newspaper, condemning the practice of taking innocent young boys and exposing them to the dangers of the Colorado River—or perhaps feeling that river rats like Bert Loper and others were not good influences on impressionable young boys. Since the *Deseret News* is owned by the L.D.S. church, its influence was considerable, and the Boy Scouts promptly dropped the program like a hot frying pan. Al Quist and other local scout leaders, such as John Cross and Moki-Mac Ellingson, objected strenuously, calling it a "boy-building experience," but to no avail. From there, it was a natural move for Quist to begin running rivers on his own. After his death, his sons Richard, Clair and Bob started their own commercial river running business which is still in existence today.

J. Frank Wright Near House Rock Rapid in the Grand Canyon, 1951

A native of Blanding, Utah, Frank Wright (second from the left) started working for Norm Nevills as a boatman, handyman, and cook shortly after World War II. Wright soon became one of Nevills favorite boatmen, with his strong, calm demeanor a fitting contrast to Nevills sometimes excitable personality. After Nevills and his wife were killed in a plane crash in September 1949, Wright and the Rigg brothers, Bob and Jim, of Grand Junction, Colorado, took over the business. It was renamed Mexican Hat Expeditions, and together they continued to offer commercial river trips on the San Juan River, as well as in Glen Canyon and the Grand Canyon. In 1957, after the Riggs had gone on to other things, Wright took on a new partner, Gaylord Staveley, but sold out to him the following year. Wright then took the job of head boatman for the Glen Canyon Salvage Survey, run by the University of Utah, and

spent the next several years shepherding scientists and students up and down Glen Canyon. In later years, after the dam was built, Wright operated the Lake Powell Ferry Service.

Otis Marston and Bill Belknap at Lake Mead, 1950

Otis "Dock" Marston began his love affair with the Colorado River in 1942, when he floated the Grand Canyon with Norm Nevills. Like many lovers, Marston soon became jealously possessive of the Colorado, thinking of it as "his" river. Marston accompanied Nevills on every Grand Canyon trip, as well as many others, from then until 1948. Although they started out as friends, their similar personalities soon began to clash, and eventually neither could stand the other. In 1948 Marston became interested in the idea of running a power-boat up the Colorado through the Grand Canyon, and devoted his considerable energies and talents to that goal for the next decade. All attempts were unsuccessful until 1960, when he was on a trip that succeeded in forcing specially designed jetboats all the way to Lees Ferry (not, however, without the loss of one of the boats and several injuries). It was the first and last such trip.

Marston is best known as the indefatigable and sometimes abrasive collector of Colorado River lore. By seeking out virtually everyone who had ever been down the Colorado River or its tributaries, he eventually amassed a vast collection of diaries, letters, clippings, photos, and films that were later deposited in the Huntington Library in California; this remains the primary source of historical information on the Colorado River. In his quest he probably made more enemies than friends. But it must be said in his defense that he was a man obsessed, and had he not collected so much data, much of it would by now be lost forever.

Bill Belknap was a photographer who lived in Boulder City, Nevada. Naturally he heard of the goings-on on the Colorado, and soon was involved in the up-river attempts. He and Marston became friends and river companions. When the gates on Glen Canyon Dam were closed and the river in the Grand Canyon dropped to a trickle, Belknap and Marston were along for a traverse in Sportyaks, seven-foot plastic dinghies, the smallest craft ever taken through the canyon. Belknap was so impressed with the small plastic boats that he pioneered their commercial use on the Green in Desolation Canyon and on the San Juan. As good a writer and photographer as he was a river runner, Belknap, with son Buzz and daughter Laura, wrote and published the Belknap river guides, still used today by thousands of river runners. He later took his turn at being president of the Western River Guides Association, a contentious group of outfitters, guides, and others interested in the river. Belknap tried to reform the boaters by doing away with free beer and rock and roll music at the conventions, but it was about like trying to run a boat up the Colorado—it's easier to go with the flow.

Katie Lee Entertaining Passengers on a 1954 Glen Canyon Trip

Katie Lee was a successful folk singer and actress when she fell in love with Glen Canyon after a trip with Mexican Hat Expeditions in the early 1950s. Often, by her own account, she "sang for her supper," paying her fare by helping out with camp chores and entertaining the passengers with her songs and guitar. Katie was stunned by the plans to dam Glen Canyon, and toured the country trying to raise the support necessary to stop its construction, all to no purpose; sentiment was too strong in favor of the dam, and Glen Canyon, despite her efforts, too little known. That's ironic in itself, for by the time that the plans for the dam were

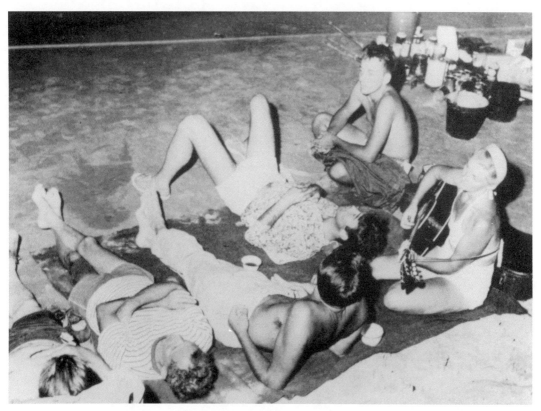

announced, river running in Glen Canyon had almost become big business. There were a number of commercial outfitters who took passengers down the river through Glen Canyon as well as increasing numbers of private boaters. Every conceivable kind of boat was used, from inner tubes to propeller- powered airboats to huge pontoon rafts. Dock Marston, ever the cynic, wryly commented that "By 1950 there was almost a need for traffic lights." Even after the dam began to go up, people continued to float Glen Canyon, now driven by an urge to see what would soon be lost forever. The damsite blocked access to Lees Ferry, the traditional take-out, but the clamorous outcry from outfitters and private river runners alike caused the Bureau of Reclamation to build a road into Kane Creek, just above the damsite, so that boaters would have an exit from the canyon.

Georgie White, the Woman of the River

Georgie White bought her first inflatable, a seven-man raft, in 1947 and took it down the flood-swollen Escalante River in southern Utah. A few years later, in 1952, she felt ready to tackle the Grand Canyon, despite the objections of many of the river runners of the time, who thought that the canyon was no place for a woman, especially one running her own boat. But Georgie was never one to let the opinions of others stop her, and with some help from Frank Wright and Jim Rigg, she became the first woman to run her own boat all the way through. Inspired, she began running what she called "share-the-expense" trips during the river season, and touring the country during the winters, showing films and signing up recruits. To accommodate a growing number of customers, she developed the G-Rig, which consisted of twenty-seven-foot pontoons lashed on either side of a thirty-three-foot pontoon, powered by an outboard motor. The raft was lashed together with a vast network of ropes, and took three days to rig at the start of the trip. The entire craft was soft; that is, there were no food boxes or other hard surfaces anywhere the passengers sat. Georgie figured that the paying customers deserved the best ride, and became famous (or infamous) for powering right down the middle of even the biggest rapids. When this resulted in passengers being thrown from the boat on one run of Crystal Rapid in the Grand Canyon, Georgie reportedly commented, "They sure don't make passengers like they used to." She was also unconcerned about the guests' comforts; meals consisted of canned food heated in boiling water and served in an inflatable bathtub, and each guest had to undergo a ceremony below Lava Falls to be initiated into "Georgie's Royal River Rats," an idea borrowed from Norm Nevills. The first-timers were blindfolded, made to kneel, and then had buckets of mud poured over them, had eggs smashed in their hair, and were swatted with a paddle. Despite this, Georgie developed a fiercely loyal following both in her crewmen—she preferred young firemen from Los Angeles, who would work for nothing—and her passengers, many of whom were (amazingly enough) repeat customers. Georgie had constant battles with the National Park Service rangers after they began to manage river running in the 1970s, and there are many stories about Georgie outfoxing the rangers when they tried to check up on her. She always did things her way, and damn the Park Service or anyone else who disagreed. Georgie ran her last trip in the Grand Canyon in the autumn of 1991, only a few months before she died at the age of 81.

Don Harris

LaPhene Harris moved from Green River, Utah, to Mexican Hat in the summer of 1938. Don Harris, as everyone called him, was the new resident engineer for the U.S.G.S., assigned the task of measuring the flow of the San Juan River every day and taking water samples to determine turbidity, silt content, and so on. Harris was from Soda Springs, Idaho, and attended the Utah State Agricultural College (now Utah State University), where he received an engineering degree in 1933, and went to work for the U.S.G.S. At Mexican Hat, he naturally got to know Norm and Doris Nevills, who ran a lodge and tourist business. He soon joined Norm for a short run on the San Juan, and when Nevills asked if he would like to go on a longer trip, Harris quickly agreed, as long as it fit into his annual-leave schedule. He helped Nevills build the three boats for the expedition, the *Wen*, the *Botany*, and the *Mexican Hat*. In return for his help, Don was to get the *Mexican Hat* at the end of the trip. They started from Green River, Utah, in June. Nevills was unsure of himself, never having run rapids as big as those in Cataract Canyon, and tensions ran high. At Lees Ferry, after agonizing over

what to do, Don Harris regretfully told Norm he couldn't go all the way through the Grand Canyon; it was still the Depression, after all, and jobs were hard to come by. Nevills held it against him the rest of his life, which says more about Norm than Don Harris. In 1939, Don made it through the Grand Canyon with, among others, Bert Loper; the next year, he floated the length of the Green River with his brother and Loper. Don was the other boatman on the trip in which Loper ran his last rapid in 1949. After World War II, Harris started a river-running business, still using the faithful *Mexican Hat*, with a partner named Jack Brennan. Their outfit was called Harris-Brennan River Expeditions, and ran trips on the Green and Colorado for many years, until Jack Brennan left to work for the Glen Canyon salvage survey. Don Harris continued in the business for several more years, followed by his son Al. Many of the men and women drawn to the Colorado River can be fairly characterized as individualistic, iconoclastic, eccentric, and often contentious; Don Harris, however, is one of the few to whom none of these labels apply. He is truly a gentleman among river runners, as difficult to achieve in its way as running Lava Falls is in another way.

Don Hatch and Shorty Burton in the Grand Canyon, 1958

By the end of the 1950s, Hatch River Expeditions had grown too large to be just a family enterprise. Bus Hatch had four sons—Gus, Don, Frank, and Ted—and every one of them worked at one time or another running boats for their dad, but he still needed more help. At first he hired local boys from Vernal and the surrounding towns, teenagers like George Wilkins, Johnny Caldwell, or Glade Ross. Later, Bus hired young men from farther afield, like Mark Garff of Salt Lake City and even kayaking champions Roger Paris of France and Walt Kirschbaum of Germany. If you were hired by Bus in those days, it was just like becoming part of his large family. He called everyone "son" and he meant it. If you needed to borrow a car or some money or be bailed out of jail, he was right there. But if you made one mistake too many, well, Bus had a quick temper and was famous for chewing out whoever deserved it, and sometimes those who didn't. Working for Bus was a good job for local teenagers. They always had money in their pockets—no place to spend it on the river—and the tanned, athletic young boatmen were irresistible to the local girls. But there was hardly time to get into trouble, since they were only in town for a day or two before they would get

a call from Bus and be back on the river. One local youth, Jesse "Shorty" Burton from up around Browns Park, worked for Bus for almost a decade and became known for the quality of his dutch-oven pies. In June 1967, just a week before Bus died, Jesse capsized a boat in Upset Rapid in the Grand Canyon and was drowned. The Hatch boatmen placed a memorial on the rocks below the rapid —a pie plate with Jesse's name and the date etched on it, in remembrance of him and those wonderful pies.

Bob and Jim Rigg

The Rigg brothers got to know the family of Norm Nevills through their father, who was a doctor in Grand Junction, Colorado, and occasionally treated the Nevills family. Norm Nevills learned to fly and had his Piper J4 serviced through Drapela Flying Service in Grand

Junction. When Jim Rigg bought out Drapela, Nevills transferred his business to Rigg Aviation. The Riggs provided air service for Nevills Expeditions, such as charters, flying passengers to and from the river, and other logistic chores. Jim and Norm soon became friends, and in 1949, Nevills asked Jim to be a boatman for a San Juan trip. After that, Jim was hooked on river running. His younger brother Bob soon followed into the river world, helping out with shuttles, both in the air and on the road. When Norm and Doris Nevills died in 1949, the Rigg brothers and Frank Wright, another Nevills boatman, took over Nevills Expeditions, renaming it Mexican Hat Expeditions.

As the co-owners of MHE, the Rigg brothers (sometimes joined by younger brother Jack) ran many trips on the San Juan and Colorado rivers. In 1950, while in Grand Canyon, they found the *Esmerelda II*, abandoned by Ed Hudson, and after some riverside repairs brought the boat successfully out of the canyon. Inspired by this, the Riggs used other powerboats in the Canyon, eventually turning the cataract boats over to Frank Wright and concentrating on powerboat trips. In 1951, after taking fourth place in the Wind River Memorial Whitewater Race in Wyoming, Jim and Bob decided to try to set a record for the fastest run through the Grand Canyon by an oar-powered boat. In one of their cataract boats, they left Lees Ferry early on the morning of June 11. Running all the rapids without stopping, they reached Mile 107 on the first night. After a few hours' rest, they continued, stopping briefly to look at Lava Falls before running it. By the time they passed Diamond Creek at Mile 225, it was dark, so they ran the rest of the rapids "by braille," as Bob remembered, rowing away from the sound of the water. That night, completely exhausted, they stopped near the Bat Caves. The next day, about a mile from Pierce Ferry, they were met by Bill Belknap and Jim Jordan, who had come to tow them the rest of the way. Total miles, about 340; total time from Lees Ferry to Separation Canyon was about thirty-eight hours. The record stood until 1983.

Art Greene's Canyon Tours Powerboat in Glen Canyon, 1962

Art Greene began taking paying customers on trips through Glen Canyon in the mid-1940s, when he was running the Marble Canyon Lodge near Lees Ferry. He would take tourists up Glen Canyon from Lees Ferry to the mouth of Aztec Creek, the access to Rainbow Bridge.

His operation, even after he began to expand following World War II, was kept low-key. There were no schedules, no assigned camps. If he happened to run into fellow river rats, he would camp then and there to visit with his friends. If the motor broke down on the way upriver, they simply drifted back down. Asked how long the trip to Rainbow Bridge would last, Art would reply, "up to a week." At first he used a small rowboat with an outboard motor, but later developed an airboat similar to those used in swampy areas. The flat-bottomed boat was powered by a 450 hp. aircraft engine, and performed beautifully, reaching speeds of 55 mph. and skimming over river and sandbars with equal ease. It used a lot of fuel, however, and worse, from the passenger's standpoint, the noise of the engine was deafening. Cotton and earplugs were standard issue on Greene's trips until 1960, when he switched to more conventional boats such as that shown here. Greene later moved on and built the Cliff Dwellers lodge, a few miles from the Navajo Bridge. Still later, using knowledge gained from conversations with Bureau of Reclamation engineers who were working on the Glen Canyon dam, Greene found a perfect site for a lodge above the high-water mark of the reservoir, leased the land, and built Wahweap Lodge, the biggest tourist facility on Lake Powell.

P. T. Reilly and Martin Litton, 1956

P. T. Reilly was working for Lockheed Aircraft Corp. in southern California when he and his wife Susie began taking river trips with Norm Nevills just after World War II. He first went as a paying passenger on the San Juan River, but Reilly was soon rowing a boat whenever he could get time off from his job. He graduated to being a boatman for Nevills, and was with him for practically the entire 1947 season, rowing the upper Green that year, soon followed by the Grand Canyon. A trained engineer, Reilly could see that with a few simple modifications, the handling characteristics of Nevills cataract boats would be greatly improved, but Nevills would have none of it. After Nevills' death in 1949, Reilly began to organize trips for his family and friends, and became a fixture in the Grand Canyon. He experimented with a number of different variations on the cataract boat theme, but after breaking all his oars during a high-water trip in 1959, he became disgusted with the boats and with river running. He pulled the boats to shore just below the Bright Angel trail, sank them by knocking holes in the bottoms with rocks, and hiked out, vowing never to return. But Reilly couldn't keep his pledge, and within a few years, he was back on the river.

Martin Litton was introduced to the Colorado River in 1951. An editor for *Sunset* magazine, he hiked into Lava Falls and watched a group of boats run that famous cataract for a story he was writing. In the next few years he became involved in the Echo Park Dam controversy in Dinosaur National Monument, and wrote a number of stories opposing the construction of the dam. In 1955, he went on a trip through the Grand Canyon with P. T. Reilly, and the next year, rowed his own boat through the canyon. Litton was especially attracted to the idea of using wooden boats—they were more stable in some situations, they were more responsive to the oars, and, more important, they imparted a feeling of closeness to the river that he didn't get in an inflatable raft. In 1962, during a vacation in the Northwest, Litton saw some MacKenzie River dories and knew at once that they would be the ideal craft for the Colorado. He had two of them built, P. T. Reilly built another (his disgust with the river since forgotten), and they took them through the Grand Canyon for the first time in 1964. Litton later founded his own river business, Grand Canyon Dories. He also became a director of the Sierra Club and was instrumental in the defeat of plans to build dams in the Grand Canyon in the mid-1960s.

Mexican Hat Expeditions, Lees Ferry to Bright Angel, 1960

Gaylord Staveley became a river runner by marriage. In 1954, he married Joan Nevills, the daughter of the late Norm Nevills. Frank Wright, who had taken over the business when Nevills was killed, invited Staveley to go on a trip down the San Juan River in 1956. That same year, he went through the Grand Canyon. Being a "midwestern farm kid," he was entranced by the Colorado River, and later wrote to Wright asking if he could be a boatman for the following season. Wright replied that he didn't need a boatman, but he did need a partner in Mexican Hat Expeditions, so in 1957 Staveley became a commercial river outfitter

and guide. The next year, Wright left to work for the Glen Canyon Salvage survey, and Gay and Joan Nevills-Staveley found themselves sole owners and operators of Mexican Hat Expeditions. They ran trips on the San Juan and in Glen Canyon and the Grand Canyon out of the old Nevills lodge in Mexican Hat, Utah, for many years. Staveley was one of the last to make the change from wooden boats to rafts; it wasn't until 1970 that he switched to inflatables. That same year he changed the name of the company to Canyoneers, Inc. Today a son, Cameron Staveley, still works in the Grand Canyon, a third-generation river runner. Another future river outfitter in this photo is Don Neff, who at the time this photo was taken was working as a boatman while a high school student on his summer vacation. He later started Dinosaur River Expeditions, offering trips on the Green and Yampa Rivers.

Jack Curry, Founder of Western River Expeditions

In the late 1950s, Hatch River Expeditions held the only official permit granted by the National Park Service to operate a commercial guide service on the Green and Yampa rivers in Dinosaur National Monument. Interest in the rivers and the monument was high; the controversy over the Echo Park dam had only recently begun to die down, and the Green and Yampa were still household words. Jack Curry of Salt Lake City decided to get into the river business. When he contacted the Park Service about getting started, however, he was told that since he didn't have a permit, he couldn't conduct tours down the river. Hatch had been on the river since the 1940s, and Curry felt that Hatch had an unfair monopoly on river running. Curry went to court and won. Curry started Western River Expeditions in 1958, running at first on the Green and Yampa, but soon expanding to the Colorado and the Grand Canyon. Western River Expeditions was, and is still, the only outfit to use the J-rig, named for him. This large craft is made of five tubes tied together to form a raft. Curry originally intended to use pontoons like everyone else, so he bought, sight unseen, a load of surplus pontoons from the government. When he unpacked the boats, however, he found to his dismay that instead of conventional pontoons, he had bought what are called snout tubes, useless, so he thought, for river running. Nonplussed, Curry and his men gaped at the heavy rolls of rubber. Running rivers teaches you to be resourceful if nothing else, though; Paul Thevenin, one of his boatmen, said, "Don't worry, Jack, we'll make a boat out of 'em," and so they did. Curry sold Western River Expeditions in 1973, but today it remains one of the largest river outfitters in the business.

A NOTE ON SOURCES

The photographs and descriptive accounts used in this book came from a variety of sources. Many are from the collections of the Special Collections Department, University of Utah, Marriott Library. Those used in particular include the papers of Norman D. Nevills, Dr. C. Gregory Crampton, Charles Kelly, and the Utah Power and Light Company, and many other smaller collections. Also used at the Marriott Library was the extensive collection of published works in the Western Americana section of Special Collections.

A second major source of information, indeed perhaps *the* source of information on the Colorado River, are the papers of Otis "Dock" Marston, deposited at the Huntington Library in San Marino, California. Marston was the self-appointed historian of the Colorado River, and his collection of photos, films, interviews, diaries, correspondence, ephemera—in fact anything that documents the history of travel on the Colorado or its tributaries—is unmatched elsewhere in the world.

The photos of the various U.S. government surveys are for the most part taken from the U.S.G.S. photo library in Denver, Colorado. Other photographs taken by government surveyors and scientists were found in the files of the U.S. Bureau of Reclamation offices in Salt Lake City, Utah. Also in Salt Lake City is the Utah State Historical Society, with its wonderful collections of river-related history, including the papers and photographs of Harry Aleson, Dr. Russell Frazier, P. T. Reilly, and the Western River Guides Association. A final source, but a good one, in Salt Lake City has been the papers of David Dexter Rust, housed in the Historical Department of the Church of Jesus Christ of Latter-day Saints.

Other photos came from various sources in Arizona, especially the photo files in the research library at the South Rim Visitors Center of Grand Canyon National Park and the Cline Library, Special Collections at Northern Arizona University, which holds the papers of the Kolb brothers and Georgie White.

A number of individuals were especially helpful in providing either stories and hard-to-find photographs, or addresses, telephone numbers, and other leads, or all of the above. These include Don Hatch, Dee Holladay, Ted Hatch, Jerry Sanderson, Charles Eggert, Philip Hyde, Bill Belknap, John Cross, Martin Litton, Marc Smith, Gaylord Staveley, Jack Curry, Ken Sleight, Richard Quist, and Roy DeSpain.

BIBLIOGRAPHY

Primary sources

Aleson, Harry. "Notes on Green River Trip, 1951." Aleson Papers, MSS B 187. Utah State Historical Society, Salt Lake City.

Belknap, Bill. Telephone conversation with author, 27 January 1986

Birney, Hoffman. "Colorado River Trip 1932." Kelly Papers, MS 100, University of Utah, Marriott Library, Special Collections

Blake, H. Elwyn. "Diary of H. Elwyn Blake, Jr." Aleson Papers, MSS B 187. Utah State Historical Society, Salt Lake City.

Burg, Amos. "Daily diary of Amos Burg from the Buzz Holmstrom-Amos Burg Colorado River Expedition." Burg Papers, MSS A 188. Utah State Historical Society, Salt Lake City.

Crampton, C. Gregory, and Steven K. Madsen. "Boating on the upper Colorado: A history of the navigational use of the Green, Colorado, and San Juan Rivers and their major tributaries." Crampton Papers, ACCN 727. University of Utah, Marriott Library, Special Collections, Salt Lake City.

Cross, John. Interview by Roy Webb, 12 March 1984. Tape Recording. University of Utah, Marriott Library, Special Collections, Salt Lake City.

Curry, Jack. Letter to author, 10 February 1986.

DeSpain, Roy. Interview by Roy Webb, 20 April 1985. Tape Recording. University of Utah, Marriott Library, Special Collections, Salt Lake City.

Eggert, Charles. Personal Communications with author, April-May 1993.

Frazier, Dr. Russell G.. "Rapids A Head." Frazier Papers, MSS B 112. Utah State Historical Society, Salt Lake City.

———. "Yampa River Trip July 1–9, 1937." Frazier Papers, MSS B 112. Utah State Historical Society, Salt Lake City.

Gardiner, W. Stewart. Interview by Roy Webb, 3 July 1984. Tape Recording. University of Utah, Marriott Library, Special Collections, Salt Lake City.

———. "River Rocks and Rapids." Roy Webb Papers, ACCN 1000. University of Utah, Marriott Library, Special Collections, Salt Lake City.

———. "A Trip down the Green River: From Henry's Fork to Jensen, Utah; October 23 to October 31 1938." Roy Webb Papers, ACCN 1000. University of Utah, Marriott Library, Special Collections, Salt Lake City.

Harris, Don. Telephone conversation with author, 9 September 1984.

———. Interview, 3 March 1989. Tape Recording. University of Utah, Marriott Library, Special Collections, Salt Lake City.

Hatch Family Papers, Hatch River Expeditions, Vernal, Utah.

Hatch, Don. Interview by Roy Webb, 10 March 1984. Tape Recording. University of Utah, Marriott Library, Special Collections, Salt Lake City.

———. Letters to author, 27 December 1985, *passim*

Hatch, Ted. Interview by Roy Webb, 13 August 1988. University of Utah Special Collections, Salt Lake City.

Hatch, Tom. Interview by Roy Webb, 15 January 1988. Tape Recording.

University of Utah, Marriott Library, Special Collections, Salt Lake City.

Holmstrom, Haldane "Buzz." "Diary of Buzz Holmstrom's trip down the Colorado Oct. 4 to Nov. 20–1937." Holmstrom Papers, MSS MIC 1389. Utah State Historical Society, Salt Lake City.

Jones, Leslie. Interview by Roy Webb. Tape Recording. University of Utah, Marriott Library, Special Collections, Salt Lake City.

Kelly, Charles. "Log of Colorado River Trip, 1932." Kelly Papers, MS 100. University of Utah, Marriott Library, Special Collections, Salt Lake City.

———. "Yampa River Trip, 1937." Kelly Papers, MS 100. University of Utah, Marriott Library, Special Collections, Salt Lake City.

———. "Colorado River Expedition, 1938." Kelly Papers, MS 100. University of Utah, Marriott Library, Special Collections, Salt Lake City.

———. "Colorado River Expedition, 1942." Kelly Papers, MS 100. University of Utah, Marriott Library, Special Collections, Salt Lake City.

Kirschbaum, Ruth. Personal Communication with author, 20 May 1993.

Litton, Martin. Telephone conversation with author, 28 January 1986.

Lee, Katie. Interview by Roy Webb, 14 April 1985. Tape Recording. University of Utah, Marriott Library, Special Collections, Salt Lake City.

Marston, Otis R. Papers. Huntington Library, San Marino California.

———. "Water Transport on the Green River." Brooks Papers, MSS B 103. Utah State Historical Society, Salt Lake City.

Nevills, Norman. Papers. MS 552, University of Utah, Marriott Library, Special Collections, Salt Lake City.

Page, F. Lemoyne. "My Trip down the Green River, 1926." Aleson Papers, MSS B 187. Utah State Historical Society, Salt Lake City.

Purdy, William M. Interview by Roy Webb, 28 August 1985. Tape Recording. University of Utah, Marriott Library, Special Collections, Salt Lake City.

Reilly, P.T. Letters to author, 11 December 1985, 3 January 1986.

Rust, David Dexter. Papers. Historical Department, Church of Jesus Christ of Latter-day Saints, Salt Lake City.

Staveley, Gaylord. Interview by Roy Webb, 13 April 1984. Tape Recording. University of Utah, Marriott Library, Special Collections, Salt Lake City.

———. Telephone conversation with author, 27 January 1986.

Stratton, Owen and Phillip Sirotkin. "The Echo Park Dam controversy and Upper Colorado River development." Photocopy. University of Utah, Marriott Library, Special Collections, Salt Lake City.

Swain, Frank. Interview by Roy Webb and Gregory C. Thompson, 2 March 1984. Tape Recording. University of Utah, Marriott Library, Special Collections, Salt Lake City.

Wilkins, George. Interview by Roy Webb, 4 November 1988. Tape Recording. University of Utah, Marriott Library, Special Collections, Salt Lake City.

Wortley, Kenneth. Letter to author, 7 February 1986.

Books

Baker, Pearl. *Trail on the Water*. Boulder: Pruett Publishing Co., n.d.

Belknap, Bill, and Buzz Belknap. *Canyonlands River Guide*. Boulder City, Nev.: Westwater Books, 1974

Belknap, Buzz. *Grand Canyon River Guide*. Evergreen, Col.: Westwater Books, 1989.

Builders of Uintah: A Centennial History of Uintah County 1872 to 1947. Springville, Utah: Art City Publishing Co., 1947.

Cook, William. *The Wen, the Botany, and the Mexican Hat: The Adventures of the First Women through the Grand Canyon, on the Nevills Expeditions*. Orangevale, Cal.: Callisto Books, 1987

Crampton, C. Gregory. *Historical Sites in Cataract and Narrow Canyons, and in Glen Canyon to California Bar*. University of Utah Anthropological Papers no. 72, Salt Lake City, Utah: University of Utah Press, 1964.

———. *Land of Living Rock*. New York: Alfred A. Knopf, 1972.

———. *Historical Sites in Glen Canyon, Mouth of Hansen Creek*. University of Utah Anthropological Papers no. 61, Salt Lake City, Utah: University of Utah Press, 1962.

———. *Historical Sites in Glen Canyon, Mouth of San Juan*. University of Utah Anthropological Papers no. 46, Salt Lake City, Utah: University of Utah Press, 1960.

———. *Outline History of the Glen Canyon Region, 1776–1922*. University of Utah Anthropological Papers no. 42, Salt Lake City, Utah: University of Utah Press, 1959.

———. *Standing Up Country: The Canyonlands of Utah and Arizona*. Salt Lake City: Peregrine Smith Books, 1983.

———. *The San Juan Canyon Historical Sites*. University of Utah Anthropological Papers no. 70, Salt Lake City, Utah: University of Utah Press, June 1964.

Crumbo, Kim. *A River Runners Guide to the History of the Grand Canyon*. Boulder: Johnson Books, 1981.

Dellenbaugh, Frederick S. *A Canyon Voyage*. New Haven: Yale University Press, 1962.

———. *The Romance of the Colorado River*. New York: G.P. Putnam's Sons, 1902.

Eddy, Clyde. *Down the World's Most Dangerous River*. New York: Frederick A. Stokes Co., 1929.

Evans, Laura. *Dinosaur River Guide*. Boulder City: Westwater Books, 1974.

—— and Buzz Belknap. *Desolation Canyon River Guide*. Boulder City: Westwater Books, 1974.

Follansbee, Robert. *The Upper Colorado River and Its Utilization*. Washington, D.C.: U.S. Government Printing Office, 1929.

Fowler, Don D., ed. *Photographed all the Best Scenery: Jack Hillers's Diary of the Powell Expeditions, 1871–1875*. Salt Lake City: University of Utah Press, 1972.

——. *Myself in the Water: The Western Photographs of John K. Hillers*. Washington, D.C.: Smithsonian Institution Press, 1989.

Fradkin, Phillip L. *A River No More: The Colorado River and the West*. New York: Alfred A. Knopf, 1981.

Freeman, Lewis R. *The Colorado River: Yesterday, Today, and Tomorrow*. New York: Dodd, Mead and Co., 1923.

——. *Down the Colorado*. New York: Dodd, Mead and Co., 1924.

Goldwater, Barry M. *An Odyssey of the Green and Colorado Rivers: The Intimate Journal of Three Boats and Nine People on a Trip down Two Rivers*. Phoenix, 1941.

Horan, James D. *Timothy O'Sullivan: America's Forgotten Photographer*. New York: Bonanza Books, 1966.

Kolb, Ellsworth L. *Through the Grand Canyon from Wyoming to Mexico*. New York: MacMillan, 1941.

LaRue, Eugene Clyde. *The Colorado River and Its Utilization*. Washington, D.C.: U.S. Government Printing Office, 1916.

Lavender, David. *River Runners of the Grand Canyon*. Tucson: Grand Canyon Natural History Association and University of Arizona Press, 1985.

Lingenfelter, Richard E. *Steamboats on the Colorado River, 1852–1916*. Tucson: University of Arizona Press, 1978.

Miser, Hugh D. *The San Juan Canyon, Southeastern Utah: A Geographic and Hydrographic Reconnaissance*. Washington, D.C.: U.S. Government Printing Office, 1924.

Neel, Susan Mae. "Utah and the Echo Park Dam Controversy." Master's thesis, University of Utah, 1980.

Newcomb, Duane, and Georgie White Clark. *Georgie White Clark: Thirty Years of River Running*. San Francisco: Chronicle Books, [n.d.]

Powell, John Wesley. *The Exploration of the Colorado River and Its Canyons*. New York: Dover Publications, 1961.

Purdy, William M. *An Outline of the History of the Flaming Gorge Area*. University of Utah Anthropological Papers no. 37, Salt Lake City, Utah: University of Utah Press, 1959.

Rusho, W. L., and C. Gregory Crampton. *Desert River Crossing: Historic Lees Ferry on the Colorado River*. Salt Lake City: Peregrine Smith Books, 1981.

Smith, Dwight L., ed. *The Photographer and the River: Franklin A. Nims' Colorado Canyon Diary*. Santa Fe: Stagecoach Press, 1967.

Stanton, Robert Brewster. *Down the Colorado*. [ed. by Dwight L. Smith]. Norman: University of Oklahoma Press, 1965.

Stanton, Robert Brewster. *The Hoskaninni Papers: Mining in Glen Canyon, 1897–1901*, ed. by C. Gregory Crampton and Dwight L. Smith, University of Utah Anthropological Papers no. 54, Salt Lake City, Utah: University of Utah Press, 1961.

——. *Colorado River Controversies*. New York: Dodd, Mead and Co., 1932.

Stegner, Wallace, ed. *This is Dinosaur: Echo Park Country and Its Magic Rivers*. New York: Alfred A. Knopf, 1955.

Stevens, Larry. *The Colorado River in the Grand Canyon: A Guide*. Flagstaff: Red Lake Books, 1983.

Stone, Julius. *Canyon Country*. New York: G. P. Putnam's Sons, 1932.

U.S. Coast and Geodetic Survey. *Annual Report of the Director, 1922*. Washington, D.C.: U.S. Government Printing Office, 1922.

Westwood, Richard E. *Rough-water Man: Elwyn Blake's Colorado River Expeditions*. Reno: University of Nevada Press, 1992.

Woodbury, Angus M., et al. *Ecological Studies of the Flora and Fauna in Glen Canyon*. University of Utah Anthropological Papers no. 40, Salt Lake City, Utah: University of Utah Press, 1959.

Woolley, Ralph R. *The Green River and Its Utilization*. Washington, D.C.: U.S. Government Printing Office, 1930

Zwinger, Ann. *Run, River, Run: A Naturalist's Journey Down One of the Great Rivers of the West*. New York: Harper and Row, 1975.

Articles

Beaman, E. O. "The Canyon of the Colorado and the Moquis Pueblos." *Appleton's Journal* 11, no. 265 (18 April 1874): 1–24

Bingham, Jay R. "Reclamation and the Colorado." *Utah Historical Quarterly* 28, no. 3 (July 1960): 233–49.

Breed, Jack. "Shooting Rapids in Dinosaur Country." *National Geographic* 105, no. 3 (March 1954): 363–90.

Case, Robert Ormand. "He Shot the Colorado Alone." *Saturday Evening Post* 210, no 35 (26 February 1938): 8–9, 34–40.

Crampton, Dr. C. Gregory. "Historic Glen Canyon." *Utah Historical Quarterly* 28, no. 3 (July 1960): 274–89.

Darrah, William Culp. "Biographical Sketches and Original Documents of the First Powell Expedition of 1869." *Utah Historical Quarterly* 15 (1947): 9–148.

Ekker, Barbara Baldwin. "Freighting on the Colorado River: Reminiscences of Virgil Fay Baldwin." *Utah Historical Quarterly* 32 (Spring 1964): 120–29.

"French Trio Reach Split Mountain on Trip to Boulder." *The Vernal [Utah] Express*, 29 September 1938.

Galloway, Nathaniel. "Through the Grand Canyon of the Colorado: Adventures by Nathan Galloway." *The Vernal [Utah] Express*, 7–21 July, 1898.

Henderson, Randall. "Boat Trip in the Canyon of Lodore." *Desert Magazine* 19 (July 1956): 4–9.

——. "Canyon Boat Ride in Utah." *Desert Magazine* 21 (December 1958): 21–25.

——. "Grand Canyon Voyage." *Desert Magazine* 11–12 (November 1947-February 1948) passim.

——. "River Trail to Rainbow Bridge." *Desert Magazine* 8 (September 1945): 17–24.

Kelly, Charles. "At Eighty-Three he is an Explorer." *Saturday Evening Post* 218 (6 May 1939): 20–21 passim.

Kirschbaum, Walter. "'Grand' Adventure." *American White Water* 6 (November 1960): 5–10

Marston, Otis R. "River Runners—Fast Water Navigation." *Utah Historical Quarterly* 28, no. 3 (July 1960): 291–308.

Purdy, William M. "Green River: Main Stem of the Colorado." *Utah Historical Quarterly* 28, no. 3 (July 1960): 250–61.

Reilly, P. T. "How deadly Is Big Red?" *Utah Historical Quarterly* 37, no. 2 (Spring 1969): 244–260.

——. "Norman Nevills: Whitewater Man of the West." *Utah Historical Quarterly* 55, no. 2 (Spring 1987): 181–200.

Rusho, W. L. ed. "River Running, 1921: The Diary of E. L. Kolb." *Utah Historical Quarterly* 37, no. 2 (Spring 1969): 269–83.

Smith, Dwight L. "The Engineer and the Canyon." *Utah Historical Quarterly* 28 no. 3 (July 1960): 262–73.

Topping, Gary. "Harry Aleson and the Place No One Knew." *Utah Historical Quarterly* 52, no. 2 (Spring 1984): 165–78.

——. "Charles Kelly's Glen Canyon Ventures and Adventures." *Utah Historical Quarterly* 55, no. 2 (Spring 1987): 120–36.

CAPTIONS AND PHOTO CREDITS

CHAPTER 1
Scientists, Surveyors, and Dam Builders

1. Major John Wesley Powell, 1867. University of Utah Marriott Library Special Collections, Salt Lake City, Utah, C. Gregory Crampton Collection, PO 197.

2. John F. Steward, member of Powell's second expedition. U.S. Geological Survey Photo Library, Denver, Colorado.

3. Frederick S. Dellenbaugh with the flag of the *Emma Dean*. University of Utah Marriott Library Special Collections, Salt Lake City, Utah, C. Gregory Crampton Collection, PO 197.

4. The start of the Denver, Colorado Canyon, and Pacific Railroad Survey, 1889. University of Utah Marriott Library Special Collections, Salt Lake City, Utah, C. Gregory Crampton Collection, PO 197.

5. U.S. Reclamation Service drill crew, 1914. U.S. Geological Survey Photo Library, Denver, Colorado.

6. W. R. Chenoweth at his plane table, 1921. U.S. Geological Survey Photo Library, Denver, Colorado.

7. U.S. Coast and Geodetic Survey crew in Glen Canyon, 1921. U.S. Bureau of Reclamation, Salt Lake City, Utah.

8. "Back of the Hat" with Kelly Trimble at work on the San Juan River, 1921. The "Hat" refers to Mexican Hat Rock, which can be seen on the upper left-hand side of the picture. U.S. Geological Survey Photo Library, Denver, Colorado.

9. Bert Loper running Slickhorn Rapid, San Juan River, 1921. U.S. Geological Survey Photo Library, Denver, Colorado.

10. Taking it easy just below Green River, Wyoming, 1922. University of Utah Marriott Library Special Collections, Salt Lake City, Utah, Utah Power and Light Collection, PO 206.

11. U.S.G.S. Grand Canyon Survey crew at Lees Ferry, July, 1923. Left to right, Leigh Lint, boatman, H. E. Blake, boatman, Frank Word, cook, Col. Claude Birdseye, chief engineer of the Topographic Branch of the U.S.G.S. and trip leader, Raymond Moore, geologist, R. W. Burchard, topographer, Lewis Freeman, boatman, and Emery Kolb, head boatman. U.S. Geological Survey Photo Library, Denver, Colorado.

12. Measuring the flow of Deer Creek Falls, 1923. U.S. Geological Survey Photo Library, Denver, Colorado.

13. Portaging Hance Rapid, 1923. U.S. Geological Survey Photo Library, Denver, Colorado.

14. Julian Steward Expedition at Lees Ferry, 1932. Left to right, Charles Kelly, Hoffman Birney, Jack Shoemaker, Dr. Julian Steward, Barney Hughes. Utah State Historical Society, Salt Lake City, Utah.

15. Cal Tech Survey party, plus Buzz Holmstrom, 1937. Left to right, Frank Dodge, John Maxson, Ian Campbell, Bob Sharp, Eddie McKee, Buzz Holmstrom, John Stark, Merrill Specer, unidentified individual. John Maxson photo, courtesy Helen Maxon Pustmueller.

16. Trouble in the Canyon of Lodore. The

Utah Fish and Game Department Survey, 1938. Roy Despain, Salem, Utah.

17. University of Utah Ecological Survey in Glen Canyon, 1954. University of Utah Marriott Library Special Collections, Salt Lake City, Utah, Angus Woodbuy Collection, PO 176.

18. Bureau of Reclamation Surveyor, Glen Cayon, 1956. U.S. Bureau of Reclamation, Salt Lake City, Utah.

19. Dr. C. Gregory Crampton in Glen Canyon. University of Utah Marriott Library Special Collections, Salt Lake City, Utah, C. Gregory Crampton Collection, PO 197.

CHAPTER 2
Prospectors

1. Jack Sumner in Glen Canyon, 1897. University of Utah Marriott Library Special Collections, Salt Lake City, Utah C. Gregory Crampton Collection, PO 197.

2. Cass Hite at Ticaboo, 1907. Utah State Historical Society, Salt Lake City, Utah.

3. William Bass, right, in his cable car, foot of Bass Trail. University of Utah Marriott Library Special Collections, Salt Lake City, Utah, C. Gregory Crampton Collection, PO 197.

4. Start of the Best Expedition, Green River, Utah, 1891. University of Utah Marriott Library Special Collections, Salt Lake City, Utah, C. Gregory Crampton Collection, PO 197.

5. Placer mining barge on the San Juan River, 1894. University of Utah Marriott Library Special Collections, Salt Lake City, Utah, Riverboats Collection, PO 063.

6. Bert Loper in the Canyon of Lodore, 1922. University of Utah Marriott Library Special Collections, Salt Lake City, Utah, Utah Power and Light Collection, PO 206.

7. Robert Brewster Stanton in Glen Canyon, 1897. University of Utah Marriott Library Special Collections, Salt Lake City, Utah, C. Gregory Crampton Collection, PO 197.

8. Freighters on the San Juan near Bluff, 1900. University of Utah Marriott Library Special Collections, Salt Lake City, Utah, Riverboats Collection, PO 063.

9. Nathaniel Galloway in Glen Canyon around 1900. Historical Department, Church of Jesus Christ of Latter-day Saints, Salt Lake City, Utah.

10. Assessment work in Glen Canyon, 1900. University of Utah Marriott Library Special Collections, Salt Lake City, Utah, C. Gregory Crampton Collection, PO 197.

11. The wreck of the Hoskaninni dredge, 1938. Utah State Historical Society, Salt Lake City, Utah.

12. Charles H. Spencer at Lees Ferry, 1910. Spencer Collection, Huntington Library, San Marino, California.

13&14. The steamboat *Charles H. Spencer* in Glen Canyon in 1911, and its remaining hull and boilers in a photograph from 1985. Kolb Collection, Northern Arizona University, Flagstaff, Arizona, and Roy Webb.

15. Charles Smith in Cataract Canyon, 1911. Kolb Collection, Northern Arizona University, Flagstaff, Arizona.

16. Rivermen on the *Undine*, early 1900s. Uni-

versity of Utah Marriott Library Special Collections, Salt Lake City, Utah, Riverboats Collection, PO 063.

17. Moab Garage and Transportation Co. launch, 1924. University of Utah Marriott Library Special Collections, Salt Lake City, Utah, Riverboats Collection, PO 063.

18. Japanese placer miners in Glen Canyon, 1938. Historical Department, Church of Jesus Christ of Latter-day Saints, Salt Lake City, Utah .

CHAPTER 3
Photographers

1. John K. Hillers at work on the Aquarius Plateau, 1873. U.S. Geological Survey Photo Library, Denver, Colorado.

2. Timothy O'Sullivan's boat, the *Picture*, Grand Canyon, 1871. Library of Congress.

3. Franklin A. Nims at Lees Ferry, Christmas 1889. University of Utah Marriott Library Special Collections, Salt Lake City, Utah, C. Gregory Crampton Collection, PO 197.

4. Charles Silver Russell on the *Utah*, 1908. Fred Harvey Corp.

5. Ellsworth and Emery Kolb on the *Defiance*, 1911. Kolb Collection, Northern Arizona University, Flagstaff, Arizona.

6. August Tadje on the *Titanic II*, 1914. Huntington Library, San Marino, California.

7. Ellsworth Kolb with camera, 1914. Kolb Collection, Northern Arizona University, Flagstaff, Arizona.

8. E. C. LaRue with panorama camera at

Vasey's Paradise, 1923. Kolb Collection, Northern Arizona University, Flagstaff, Arizona.

9. Chester and Kenneth Wortley in Glen Canyon, 1924. Courtesy Kenneth Wortley.

10. Clyde Eddy Party, Grand Canyon, 1927. Courtesy Helen Eddy.

11. Cast and crew of *Bride of the Colorado*, 1927. Courtesy J. R. Bray.

12. *Denver Post* "Exploration" of the Yampa River, 1928. The estimate of flow is about 1,000 cfs. *Denver Post* photograph.

13. Lining Soap Creek Rapid, 1934. Utah State Historical Society, Salt Lake City, Utah, Dr. Russell G. Frazier Papers.

14. The *Deseret News* crew on the Yampa, 1937. Left to right, Henry Millecam, Hack Miller, Alt Hatch, Cap Mowrey, Charles Kelly. Utah State Historical Society, Salt Lake City, Utah, Dr. Russell G. Frazier Papers.

15. The Burg-Holmstrom Party at Camp, 1938. Amos Burg photograph, courtesy Cort Conley.

16. Genevieve DeColmont filming her husband in his kayak, 1938. University of Utah Marriott Library Special Collections, Salt Lake City, Utah, Antoine DeSeyne photograph.

17. The Fox-Movietone Rainbow Bridge Expedition in Glen Canyon, 1945. Left to right, Norm Nevills, Wayne McConkie, Steve Fulmer [?] Reek, Ray Zeiss, Jack Kuhne, and [?] Lehman. Courtesy Steve Fulmer.

18. Al Morton on the *Moviemaker*. Utah State Historical Society, Salt Lake City, Utah.

19. Les Jones at the Oars of *Honey—The Rapids Queen*. Courtesy Les Jones.

20. Fred Wood, Charles Eggert, and Bruce Lium. Courtesy Philip Hyde.

CHAPTER 4
Adventurers

1. The *Major Powell* after being abandoned, 1894. University of Utah Marriott Library Special Collections, Salt Lake City, Utah, Riverboats Collection, PO 063.

2. Julius F. Stone at Separation Canyon, 1939. Utah State Historical Society, Salt Lake City, Utah.

3. Seymour Dubendorff at Split Mountain Canyon, 1909. Raymond Cogswell photograph.

4. Ellsworth Kolb on the Grand River, 1916. University of Utah Marriott Library Special Collections, Salt Lake City, Utah, C. Gregory Crampton Collection, PO 197.

5. Todd-Page Party, August 1926. Left to right, Curley Hale, F. Lemoyne Page, Og West, H. E. Blake, Web Todd. Huntington Library, San Marino, California.

6. Bessie and Glen Hyde at Hermit Camp, 1928. Huntington Library, San Marino, California, photo by Aldolph Sutro.

7. Doc Inglesby in Glen Canyon. Utah State Historical Society, Salt Lake City, Utah, Dr. Russell G. Frazier Papers.

8. The "Dusty Dozen," 1934. Left to right, Alt Hatch, Cap Mowrey, Russ Frazier, Clyde Eddy, Frank Swain, Bill Fahrni, Bus Hatch. Utah State Historical Society, Salt Lake City, Utah, Dr. Russell G. Frazier Papers

9. The Stone-Frazier party in Glen Canyon, 1938. Utah State Historical Society, Salt Lake City, Utah, Dr. Russell G. Frazier Papers.

10. Haldane "Buzz" Holmstrom and Lois Jotter, 1938. University of Utah Marriott Library Special Collections, Salt Lake City, Utah, Norman D. Nevills Collection, PO 341.

11. The French Trio. University of Utah Marriott Library Special Collections, Salt Lake City, Utah, Antoine DeSeyne photograph.

12. Barry Goldwater at the Utah-Arizona border, 1940. Courtesy Barry Goldwater.

13. Nevills Expeditions, Grand Canyon, 1941. University of Utah Marriott Library Special Collections, Salt Lake City, Utah, Norman D. Nevills Collection, PO 341.

14. Louis West marooned at Separation Canyon, 1940. Utah State Historical Society, Salt Lake City, Utah, Harry Aleson Collection.

15. Alexander "Zee" Grant in the Grand Canyon, 1941. University of Utah Marriott Library Special Collections, Salt Lake City, Utah, Norman D. Nevills Collection, PO 341.

16. Georgie White and Harry Aleson, 1945. Utah State Historical Society, Salt Lake City, Utah, Harry Aleson Collection.

17&18. Willie Taylor at Jensen, Utah 1947, and the plaque marking Willie's grave in Marble Canyon. Both Otis Marston photographs, Huntington Library, San Marino, California.

19. Ed Hudson on the *Esmerelda II*, 1949. Otis Marston photograph, Huntington Library, San Marino, California.

20. John and Leo Krusack at Lees Ferry, 1952. Leo Krusack photograph.

21. Bill Beer and John Daggett at Lake Mead, April 1955. Bill Beer photograph, Huntington Library, San Marino, California.

22. The End of the First Friendship Cruise, 1957. University of Utah Marriott Library Special Collections, Salt Lake City, Utah, Green River, Utah Collection, PO 062.

23. Walter Kirschbaum. Courtesy Ruth Kirschbaum.

24. Jon Hamilton drives the *Kiwi* to the top of Vulcan Rapid. Photograph by Bill Belknap.

CHAPTER 5
Outfitters

1. David Dexter Rust at the Bright Angel tramway, 1903. Historical Department, Church of Jesus Christ of Latter-day Saints, Salt Lake City, Utah.

2. The stern-wheeler *Cliff Dweller*, 1905. University of Utah Marriott Library Special Collections, Salt Lake City, Utah, Riverboats Collection, PO 063.

3. The steamboat *Comet* on the upper Green River, 1908. University of Utah Marriott Library Special Collections, Salt Lake City, Utah, Riverboats Collection, PO 063.

4. Don and Bus Hatch on the Yampa River. Courtesy Don Hatch.

5. Doris, Joan, and Norman Nevills. University of Utah Marriott Library Special Collections, Salt Lake City, Utah, Norman D. Nevills Collection, PO 341.

6. Harry Aleson (left) and Ralph Badger at Hite, 1946. Utah State Historical Society, Salt Lake City, Utah.

7. Kent Frost, camp cook, at Lava Falls, 1947. Otis Marston photograph, Huntington Library, San Marino, California.

8. Reynolds-Hallacy cataract boat, 1947. P. T. Reilly photograph.

9. John Cross, Explorer Scout leader, in Glen Canyon, 1947. Courtesy John Cross.

10. Moki-Mac—Malcolm Ellingson. Courtesy Moki-Mac River Expeditions.

11. Albert Quist on the Yampa, 1958. Courtesy Moki-Mac River Expeditions.

12. J. Frank Wright, second from left, in the Grand Canyon, 1951. Paul Wright photograph, Huntington Library, San Marino, California.

13. Otis Martston and Bill Belknap at Lake Mead, 1950. Cliff Segerbloom photograph.

14. Katie Lee (with guitar) entertaining passengers on a 1954 Glen Canyon trip. Courtesy Tad Nichols.

15. Georgie White. Teresa Yates photograph.

16. Don Harris. University of Utah Marriott Library Special Collections, Salt Lake City, Utah, Norman D. Nevills Collection, PO 341.

17. Don Hatch and Shorty Burton, Grand Canyon, 1958. Courtesy Don Hatch.

18. Bob and Jim Rigg. Courtesy Bob Rigg.

19. Art Greene's Canyon Tours in Glen Canyon, 1962. U.S. Bureau of Reclamation.

20. P. T. Reilly (second from left, standing) and Martin Litton (third from left, standing), 1956. Courtesy Martin Litton.

21. Mexican Hat Expeditions, 1960. Left to right, back row, Don Goldman, Ralph Woollett, John Harper, Glen Goldman, Gaylord Staveley, Don Neff, front, Melvin L. Goldman. Courtesy Gaylord Staveley.

22. Jack Curry. Courtesy Jack Curry.

INDEX